TCHAÏKOVSKY

ENCORE MUSIC EDITIONS
Reprints of outstanding works on music

TCHAÏKOVSKY

A Short Biography

by

GERALD ABRAHAM

HYPERION PRESS, INC.
Westport, Connecticut

Published in 1945 by Duckworth, London
Hyperion reprint edition 1979, 1993
Library of Congress Catalog Number 78-58996
ISBN 0-88355-672-3
Printed in the United States of America

Library of Congress Cataloging in Publication Data
Abraham, Gerald Ernest Heal, 1904–
    Tchaïkovsky : a short biography.

    (Core collection reprints)
    Reprint of the 1945 ed. published by Duckworth,
London.
    "Tchaïkovsky's compositions"
    Bibliography
    1. Chaikovskii, Petr Il'ich, 1840–1893.
2. Composers—Russia—Biography.
ML410.C4A53   1979   780'.92'4   [B]   78-58996
ISBN 0-88355-672-3

CONTENTS

CHRONOLOGY

1840....Born at Votkinsk (Vyatka Government), April 25/May 7.[1]

1845....First music lessons.

1850....At preparatory school in Petersburg.

1852....Enters School of Jurisprudence.

1854....Mother's death.

1859–63.Clerk in Ministry of Justice.

1861....First visit to the West; takes private lessons from Zaremba.

1862–65.Student at Petersburg Conservatoire.

1866–78.Professor of Harmony at Moscow Conservatoire.

1868....First Symphony performed (February 3rd/15th); attracted by Desirée Artôt.

1869....*The Voevoda* produced (January 30th/ February 11th).

1871–76.Music critic of *Russky Vedomosti*.

1873....Second Symphony performed (January 26th/February 7th).

1874....*The Oprichnik* produced (April 12th/24th).

1875....First performances of Third Symphony (November 7th/19th) and B flat minor Piano Concerto (November 21st/ December 3rd).

---

[1] The first date is the Russian one, 'old style'; the second the equivalent according to the Western calendar.

1876.... At Bayreuth; first performance of *Vakula the Smith* (November 24th/December 6th).

1877.... Beginning of friendship with Nadezhda von Meck; marriage to Antonina Ivanovna Milyukova (July 6th/18th); attempted suicide; flight to Petersburg (September 24th/October 6th).

1878.... Fourth Symphony performed (November 25th/December 7th).

1879.... First (student) performance of *Eugene Onegin* (March 17th/29th).

1881.... First (professional) performance of *Onegin* (January 11th/23rd) and of *The Maid of Orleans* (February 13th/25th).

1884.... Production of *Mazeppa* (February 3rd/15th).

1885.... Takes a house of his own at Maidanovo.

1888.... First European tour as conductor; move to Frolovskoe; Fifth Symphony performed (November 5th/17th).

1890.... Production of *The Sleeping Beauty* (January 3rd/15th and *Queen of Spades* (December 7th/19th); end of friendship with Mme. von Meck.

1891.... American tour.

1892.... Move to Klin; *Iolanta* and *Nutcracker* produced (December 6th/18th).

1893.... *Pathétique* Symphony performed (October 16th/28th); death (October 25th/November 6th).

INTRODUCTION

MANY composers have written music more interesting than Tchaïkovsky's; none, it is fairly
safe to say, has been more interesting as a man.
Far from being a great man, he was not even a
great personality, like Wagner, or a striking one,
like Berlioz; some of his fellow-Russians—for
instance, Balakirev and Skryabin—led far more
fantastic lives. But Tchaïkovsky was more puzzling than any of them; his character offers more
interesting material to the amateur psychologist
than any musician from Jubal to the present day.
The contrast between the outward man seen by
his acquaintances (the pleasant companion, somewhat shy, but still a polished man of the world)
and the real man (the neurotic, the secret drinker)
is striking enough to begin with. 'His manner
was simple and natural and he always appeared
to speak with warmth and sincerity', says Rimsky-
Korsakov. And intellectually he was simple; he
seems to have been completely lacking in petty
affectations; he did try desperately all his life to
be sincere. Yet many instances in his correspondence betray that it was his habit to say one thing
to one person and something very different to
someone else, and in everyday life, often in quite
trivial matters, he seems never to have shrunk
from a convenient lie (often naïvely confessing to

it later), and it is hardly too much to say that his whole outward life was a façade carefully built up and desperately preserved, to give the world a certain impression and conceal his true nature. He once confessed to Mme. von Meck that he dreaded the consequence of fame—interest in his person—and was almost tempted to evade it by repressing his artistic ambitions.

In this short biography—a revised version of that originally published in *Masters of Russian Music*, a book written in collaboration with M. D. Calvocoressi—I have tried to combine a picture of that 'true nature' with a narrative of the outward facts of Tchaïkovsky's life, but space limitations have precluded musical criticism of even the most superficial kind.

The list of Tchaïkovsky's works at the end is (I believe) the most complete and (I hope) the most accurate yet published.

CHAPTER I

1840–66

Parentage and birth – early education – sensitiveness to music – preparatory school in Petersburg – at the School of Jurisprudence – mother's death – first attempts at composition – influence of Mozart and Italian opera – becomes clerk in Ministry of Justice – young man-about-town – influence of Piccioli – first printed composition – visits Western Europe – studies thorough-bass with Zaremba – becomes student at Petersburg Conservatoire – resigns from Ministry of Justice – friendship with Laroche – Anton Rubinstein – overture to Ostrovsky's *Storm* – *Dance of the Serving Maidens* – appointed Professor of Harmony in Moscow Conservatoire – failure of leaving cantata.

In the year 1833 a thirty-eight-year-old Inspector in the Department of Mines, Ilya Petrovich Tchaïkovsky, took as his second wife a girl in her early twenties, Alexandra Assière, the daughter of a French emigrant of whom we know nothing except that he was epileptic. (It is possible that the French grandfather of the composer of the *1812* overture was, like Cui's father, part of the jetsam left in Russia from the wreck of Napoleon's army.) Ilya Tchaïkovsky, an official of very moderate ability and intelligence, was in 1837 put in charge of the important mines at Votkinsk in the Vyatka Government; and the following year Alexandra bore him a first son, Nicholas. (He already had a daughter, Zinayda, by his first wife, a German.) On April 25th/May 7th, 1840,[1]

[1] This not unimportant date is given incorrectly in the abridged English edition of Modest Tchaïkovsky's *Life and Letters* of his famous brother.

came a second son, Peter, or 'Pierre' as his mother called him. In less than two years a daughter, Alexandra, arrived; in 1844, another son, Hippolyte; finally, in 1850, twins, Anatol and Modest.

Peter's education began at the end of 1844, when his mother engaged a young French governess, Fanny Dürbach, for Nicholas and her niece, Lydia, who was also a member of their household. He insisted on sharing their lessons, and at six is reputed to have been able to read French and German fluently. At seven he was writing verses in French. For the rest, he was slovenly, imaginative and excessively sensitive. Mlle. Dürbach, who outlived her famous pupil, told Modest half a century later that 'Peter's sensitiveness was simply boundless and one had to handle him very carefully. A mere trifle would wound him. He was a "porcelain" child. There could be no question of punishing him; he would take to heart the least criticism—a single word of reproof, such as other children would take no notice of—and be alarmingly upset by it. . . . One day, turning over the pages of his atlas and coming to the map of Europe, he at once began to cover Russia with kisses and spat on the other parts of Europe. When I told him he ought to be ashamed of himself . . . and reminded him that he was spitting on his Fanny, since she was a Frenchwoman, he replied: "There's no need to scold me. Didn't you see that I covered France with my left hand?" . . . Left to himself, he preferred to play the piano, or read or write poetry'. His governess preserved some of the precocious verses in his old exercise-books, one or two in Russian, the rest in French—religious, patriotic and dreadfully sentimental.

Neither Mlle. Dürbach nor either of the boy's parents was musical, but at five he began to have lessons from a Russian girl. We know nothing of her, except that in three years her pupil could read at sight as well as she could, which may or may not be a tribute to her ability as a teacher. Even before these first piano lessons he had shown intense delight in the tunes played by an 'orchestrion'—airs from *Don Giovanni* and the operas of Bellini and Donizetti, which he managed to pick out on the piano—and his governess has recorded that music always had an extraordinarily exciting effect on his nervous system. Once, after a party, at which there had been music, she found him sitting up in bed, his eyes feverish and glittering, crying, 'Oh, this music, this music! Take it away! It's here in my head and it won't let me go to sleep!' A Polish visitor having introduced little Pierre to Chopin's mazurkas, the boy taught himself to play two of them.

In 1848 Ilya Tchaïkovsky retired from the government service with the rank of major-general, and the family left Votkinsk, first for Moscow, then for St. Petersburg. Fanny Dürbach was dismissed and Nicholas and Peter were sent to a school where they were absurdly overworked. Peter also had a few music-lessons from a rather better teacher, and was taken more than once to the opera, though the only work he remembered was *A Life for the Tsar*. But within a month or two both boys had measles, which affected Peter's health so seriously that he was forbidden all work for nearly six months. By that time (June, 1849) his father had obtained a private appointment as manager of some mines at Alapev, and the family (except Nicholas who was left at school in Petersburg) moved to that small provincial town. Peter's education was put into the indifferent hands of his half-sister, and he quickly grew morose and idle, making his mother 'cry with vexation', as she wrote to Mlle. Dürbach. Only with the arrival of a new governess, Anastasya Petrova, did he begin to behave himself. But his musical education was quite neglected, as his parents considered that music had an 'unhealthy' effect on him. But he used to amuse himself with improvisation; by his own account, his head was at that time always full of musical sounds.

In August, 1850, Peter's mother took him to Petersburg, where he entered a preparatory school. The memory of the October day when she left him—and he had to be separated from her literally by force—remained with Tchaïkovsky to the end of his life. So, perhaps, did the effect of the year or so of agonizing homesickness which followed. Peter with his brother, who was being prepared for the School of Mining Engineers, boarded with family friends, but nothing seemed to compensate the moody, sensitive child for the loss of his parents. It was not till May, 1852, when his father retired on his savings and pension, and the family settled in Petersburg, that the boy's life became a little happier. At the same time he entered the School of Jurisprudence, the School which had earlier produced the composer Alexander Serov and the art critic Vladimir Stassov, though music was no longer cultivated in its classrooms as it had been in their days. But this period of happiness was shortlived. The mother's death from cholera in July, 1854, broke up the Tchaïkovsky household, for the older half-sister was already married. Ilya made his home in 1855 with his brother, and the children were sent to various schools. In 1858, in consequence of the loss of badly invested savings, however, he was obliged to re-enter the civil service as Director of the Technological Institute. Seven years later —at seventy—he married for a third time.

Curiously enough, Peter's very first attempt at definite composition dates from the month of his mother's death, for in July, 1854, he wrote to a now-forgotten poet, V. I. Olkhovsky, about a libretto for a one-act lyric opera *Hyperbole*, which he thought of composing—naturally, without the faintest idea of how to set about it. And the following month, at Oranienbaum, the fourteen-year-old wrote his first known composition, a little *Valse dédiée a m-lle. Anastasie*, i.e. to Anastasya Petrova, his former governess. None of Peter's comrades at the School of Jurisprudence were musical, but his mother's sister, an amateur singer

of some ability, introduced him to a good deal of
the popular operatic music of the day. Again it
was *Don Giovanni*, of which she had a vocal score,
which made by far the deepest impression on him.
In later life, Tchaïkovsky always attributed his
real initiation into the world of music to Mozart
—and to *Don Giovanni* in particular. The boy
appears to have had an extraordinarily good
soprano voice; he had a few singing lessons from
Lomakin, who, a few years later, was to join
Balakirev in founding the Free School of Music;
and his aunt encouraged him to tackle the florid
bravura airs of Rossini and the other Italians.
As a pianist he was still merely an exceedingly
diffident amateur, willing to play for dancing,
however, and fond of improvisation when assured
that he was quite alone. But he does not appear
to have written anything between 1854 and 1860,
with the exception of a setting of a poem by Mey,
which, according to Modest, was 'a purely ama-
teurish affair without the least trace of talent'.
He had a few lessons from one Bekker, more from
a German, Rudolf Kündinger, who as he confessed
later 'had no real faith in Peter Ilyich's gift for
music'. As for his studies at the School of Jurisprudence, Tchaïkovsky distinguished himself in
no way, except as a particularly bad mathema-
tician. Neither his professors nor his fellow-pupils
made any deep impression on him, though he was
friendly with Apukhtin, who soon acquired some
reputation as a minor poet. The most intimate
of Tchaïkovsky's school friends was V. S. Adamov,

afterwards a brilliant jurist, fond of music, but no
musician.   On May 13th/25th, 1859, Tchaïkovsky
left the school and entered the Ministry of Justice
as a first-class clerk.

The new official must have been one of the
most inefficient members even of the Russian civil
service of that period.   He quite forgot afterwards
what his duties had been.   Tchaïkovsky always
had a habit of absentmindedly tearing little bits
off concert-programmes and the like, and chewing
them; and there is a legend that on one occasion
he partly devoured an official document in this
way.   Nor was he dreaming, so far as we know,
of an artistic career, fond though he was of music.
It was just that he was an idle young man-about-
town, a frequenter of the theatre (particularly the
ballet and the Italian opera), egotistical and
slightly patronizing toward his father and the
other elder members of his family.   The high-
water marks of his musical taste, other than *Don
Giovanni*, were *Der Freischütz* and *A Life for the
Tsar*.   For the last year or two he had been
intimate with an unpleasant character named
Piccioli, an Italian singing-master who 'dyed his
hair and painted his face' and was reputed to be
a good deal older than the fifty years which he
modestly claimed.   Just what part Piccioli played
in Tchaïkovsky's private life we shall never know,
but musically he was a violent admirer of the
works of his fellow-countrymen—and nothing else.
He equally detested Beethoven and Glinka.   It
was perhaps under his influence that Tchaïkovsky

wrote his first printed composition: '*Mezza Notte*': *Romance pour soprano ou ténor avec accompagnement de piano*, a setting of Italian words to quasi-Italian music. The song, printed in 1860 or 1861, probably at the composer's expense, and issued by Leibrock's music-shop, the *Musée Musical*, was unknown till 1926, when a copy was found in the publisher Jurgenson's archives.

It may have been this effusion which suddenly gave Ilya Tchaïkovsky the notion that his son might do something as a musician after all. 'At supper they spoke of my musical talent', Peter wrote in March, 1861, to his sister Alexandra.[1] 'Father declared it was not yet too late for me to become an artist. If only that were really true! But it's like this: even if I actually had any talent, it can hardly be developed now. They've made an official of me, though a bad one; I'm doing my best to improve and attend to my duties more conscientiously; and at the same time I'm to study thorough-bass!'

One consequence of his sister's marriage was that he began to take an interest in the twins, ten years younger than himself, whom he had hitherto ignored. They worshipped him and he now became extremely fond of them, trying (as he said) 'to give them a substitute for a mother's love and care'. During his first trip abroad, his letters home were full of inquiries about 'Modi'

---

[1] She had recently married L. V. Davïdov, son of a prominent Decembrist who had been a friend of Pushkin's, and had gone to live in the Kiev Government.

and 'Toly'. During this expedition (July–
September, 1861) he visited Berlin, Hamburg,
Brussels, London (which he found 'very interesting, but gloomy') and Paris, which delighted him.
But the trip was spoiled by 'painful misunder-
standings' with his travelling companion, a friend
of his father's for whom he had to act as inter-
preter. In a letter to his sister, after his return,
he says: 'If ever I started on a colossal piece of
folly, it was this journey. . . . I spent more money
than I ought to have, and got nothing useful for
it. D'you see now what a fool I've been? But
don't scold me. I've behaved like a child—that's
all. . . . You know I have a weakness; directly
I get any money I squander it on pleasure; it's
vulgar and stupid, I know; but it seems to be a
part of my nature. . . . What can I expect from
the future? It's terrible to think of it. I know
that sooner or later I shall no longer be able to
battle with life's difficulties; till then, however, I
intend to enjoy it and to sacrifice everything to
that enjoyment. I have been pursued by mis-
fortune during the last fortnight; official work—
very bad. . . . P.S. I've begun to study thorough-
bass and am making good progress. Who knows?
Perhaps in three years' time you'll be hearing my
operas and singing my arias'. Six weeks later he
writes again that 'with my fairly respectable talent
(I hope you won't take that for bragging) it would
be foolish not to try my fortune in this direction'
(i.e. music). 'I am fearful only of my own
backbonelessness. In the end my indolence will

conquer; but if it doesn't I promise you that
something will come of me. Fortunately, it's not
yet too late'.

These 'studies in thorough-bass' were private
lessons from the pedantic Polish theorist, N. I.
Zaremba. But the twenty-one-year-old dilet-
tante, after beginning to study 'very superficially,
like a true amateur', was inspired by Zaremba to
work diligently, cutting adrift from all his old
friends except Apukhtin and Adamov and devoting himself to his harmony-exercises and the twins.
(Both his other brothers had left Petersburg,
Nicholas following his father in the Mining
Department, Hippolyte entering the navy.)
In 1862 an 'unjust' promotion over his head
extinguished whatever flickering enthusiasm
Tchaïkovsky had managed to work up for his
official duties. And in September the Russian
Music Society opened its new Conservatoire of
Music, with Anton Rubinstein as its principal.
Zaremba became a member of the staff—he
succeeded Rubinstein as head of the Conservatoire
in 1867—and Tchaïkovsky followed his teacher,
attending two classes a week, for he now added
strict counterpoint to his harmony studies. He
had already 'come to the conclusion that sooner
or later I shall exchange the civil service for
music. Don't imagine that I dream of ever
becoming a great artist. . . .' (Though he *was*
dreaming of it, even boasting to Nicholas that
'even if I don't turn out to be a Glinka, you will
be proud one of these days to be my brother'.)

'I only want to do the work for which I feel I have a vocation. Whether I become a celebrated composer or a poor music-teacher—it's all the same. . . . My conscience will be clear. . . . Of course, I shan't resign my post till I'm quite sure that I'm not an official but an artist'.

However, it took him less than six months to come to that conclusion, for in April, 1863, he decided to resign from the Ministry of Justice and concentrate on his musical studies. It was a risky step, for his father was by no means well off and could give him nothing but board and lodging, a small bed-sitting-room. But he cut down all his amusements and renounced the theatre; Rubinstein got him a few private pupils; and he looked forward to obtaining perhaps an assistant professorship at the Conservatoire before long. He was confident, he told Alexandra, that by the time he had finished the course he would be at least a good musician, able to earn a living. 'The professors are satisfied with me and say that with the necessary zeal I shall do very well indeed. I don't say that boastfully—it's not my nature—but frankly and without false modesty. I dream of coming to you for a whole year, when my studies are finished, and composing a big work in your quiet surroundings. Then—out into the wide world'.

At the very beginning of his Conservatoire days, in the piano-class of Mussorgsky's old teacher, Herke, Tchaïkovsky had made the acquaintance of Hermann Laroche, a German-Russian lad five

years younger than himself, afterwards notorious
as a critic, 'a Russian copy of Eduard Hanslick'
as Rimsky-Korsakov said.   Laroche was a bitter
antagonist of the Balakirev group of composers,
but he became Tchaïkovsky's intimate and lifelong
friend.   From the first, Tchaïkovsky attached
great importance to his judgement, and we are
indebted to Laroche for most of our information
concerning Tchaïkovsky's Conservatoire period.

In September, 1863, the once foppish Tchaïkovsky, now long-haired and distinctly shabby,
began to study form with Zaremba and entered
Rubinstein's instrumentation class.   Zaremba had
never been more than a mere teacher to him; he
was antagonized by Zaremba's contempt for
Mozart and Glinka, while Zaremba's own gods,
Beethoven and Mendelssohn, never had much
attraction for Tchaïkovsky.   But with Rubinstein,
a much younger man, still only in his early
thirties, it was different.   Tchaïkovsky disliked
his compositions and made fun of his bad Russian,
but according to Laroche he was completely under
his spell as a man and teacher and would take
any amount of trouble to please him, sometimes
sitting up all night over the scores he had to
submit: orchestral arrangements of such things
as the scherzo from Weber's Piano Sonata,
Op. 39, the first movement of the *Kreutzer* Sonata,
and some of Schumann's *Etudes Symphoniques*.
But he seldom, if ever, earned much reward in
the way of praise, for Rubinstein was a hard
taskmaster and he failed to see that Tchaïkovsky

was specially gifted. To the end, the man whose praise Tchaïkovsky would have valued more than that of anyone else disliked his music. Just before he came under Rubinstein's direct influence, he and Laroche also made the acquaintance of Rubinstein's enemy, Serov. Tchaïkovsky attended the rehearsals of Serov's opera *Judith*, which he still admired long afterward, but he soon took a dislike to Serov personally. Among other new friends of the same period were Alexandra's two musical sisters-in-law, Elisabeth and Vera Davïdova, who, with their aged mother,[1] came to live in the northern capital.

In addition to his more serious studies, Tchaïkovsky took a few organ lessons and learned the flute in order to play in the Conservatoire orchestra. With the same orchestra he had his first experience of conducting. According to Laroche: 'He declared that having to stand at the raised desk in front of the orchestra produced such a nervous terror that he felt all the time his head must fall from his shoulders; in order to prevent such a catastrophe, he kept his left hand under his chin and conducted only with his right. Incredible as it seems, this illusion lasted for years'.

In the summer of 1864, during a holiday in the country, Tchaïkovsky wrote his first orchestral

---

[1] Mme. Davïdova, a Frenchwoman, had been frivolous and coquettish in her younger days and evidently made amorous advances to Pushkin, when he was her husband's guest at Kamenka. The poet alludes to her very disrespectfully in some of his verses.

work. Rubinstein usually gave his composition
pupils a biggish holiday task and Tchaïkovsky
was told to write an overture. Now Tchaïkovsky,
though he disliked what little he knew of Liszt and
Wagner, had been attracted to programme-music
by the overtures of the now - forgotten Henri
Litolff, a composer who was also admired by
Balakirev and Borodin. Accordingly, instead of
a harmless academic piece in sonata-form, his
exercise took the shape of a highly dramatic
concert-overture [1] with a programme based on
Ostrovsky's tragedy, *The Storm*, a play which had
appeared three or four years before and completely
enthralled him. This in itself was enough to
annoy Rubinstein. And it was scored for a very
'modern' orchestra, including harp, *cor anglais* and
tuba—extravagances of which Anton strongly dis-
approved. Amusingly enough, Tchaïkovsky was
in such a hurry for Rubinstein to see it that he
posted the score to Laroche with a request that *he*
would take it to Rubinstein. And so it came
about that it was Laroche who had to bear the
brunt of the outraged purist's wrath. The next
composition of which we hear is an orchestral
Dance of the Serving Maidens (afterwards used in the
opera *The Voevoda*) which was played at Pavlovsk
during the summer of 1865, by Johann Strauss,
the Strauss of the *Blue Danube*.

Tchaïkovsky spent that summer with his
brother-in-law Davïdov, on the latter's estate of
Kamenka in the Kiev Government. Kamenka

---

[1] Published posthumously as Op. 76.

had poetic and historical associations that might well have stirred an imaginative man. It had been a favourite meeting-place of the Decembrist conspirators, and Pushkin had stayed there forty-five years before and written part of his *Prisoner of the Caucasus* under its hospitable roof. But Tchaïkovsky had learned his lesson. He annoyed Rubinstein with no Pushkinian symphonic poem. Two overtures were written that summer, besides a translation of Gevaert's recently published *Traité d'Instrumentation* for Rubinstein, but they were both perfectly innocuous works, in C minor and F, though the former embodied a certain amount of material salvaged from *The Storm*. Tchaïkovsky returned to Petersburg in August with his two overtures (of which only the second was orchestrated, so far) and an Ukrainian folk-song, which he had heard sung every day by women in the garden at Kamenka and which he proceeded to use in the slow movement of a String Quartet in B flat.

Tchaïkovsky's position was anything but pleasant that autumn. His eyes were giving him a great deal of trouble, while his rooms were uncomfortable and he kept flitting from one apartment to another. Nor was he by any means as confident as he had been two years before of his ability to earn a living on leaving the Conservatoire. He even thought—and some of his friends encouraged the idea—of returning to the civil service. But an unexpected way out presented itself. Rubinstein's younger brother Nicholas (a

man only five years Tchaïkovsky's senior), assisted
by a still younger man, the twenty-nine-year-old
publisher Jurgenson, was founding a Conservatoire
of Music in Moscow. He wanted a Professor of
Harmony, but being unable to pay more than a
miserable pittance—fifty rubles (say £5) a month!
—sounded Anton as to the capabilities of any of
his senior students for the post. Anton recom-
mended Tchaïkovsky and in November the latter
accepted.

But the rather callow professor of twenty-five
did not leave the Petersburg Conservatoire under
the happiest auspices. True, his Quartet was
played at a pupils' concert. But he must have
been dissatisfied with it, for he destroyed all but
the first movement and used his folk-song a few
months later in a *Scherzo à la russe* for piano, his
Op. 1, No. 1. The Overture in F, which the
Conservatoire orchestra played under his baton,
pleased him better, for in February he rescored it
for a larger orchestra and it was played publicly
in both Petersburg and Moscow. But his leaving
cantata, a modest attempt to rival Beethoven in
setting Schiller's *An die Freude* for soloists, chorus
and orchestra, was a failure. (The subject was
Rubinstein's choice, not Tchaïkovsky's, and a
quarter of a century later the composer very
firmly refused to allow Jurgenson to publish the
work.) The cantata was performed at the prize
distribution on December 31st, 1865/January 12th,
1866—just twelve days after the first performance
of Rimsky-Korsakov's First Symphony—in the

presence of the directors of the Russian Music Society, the Director of the Imperial Chapel and the conductors of the Imperial Theatres, but in the absence of the composer. Tchaïkovsky's nerve had given way at the last moment and he could not bring himself to face the customary *viva voce* examination in public. Rubinstein was not only so annoyed that he at first threatened to withhold the diploma, but afterwards declined to perform the cantata at an R.M.S. concert unless it was drastically revised. Indeed, the unlucky cantata had the distinction of being condemned by *all* parties, one not easily achieved in Petersburg in those days. A work which compelled Anton Rubinstein, Cui *and* Serov to agree must, one feels, have possessed very unusual qualities. Only the unhappy composer's bosom friend thought otherwise.

In his first letter to Tchaïkovsky in Moscow, Laroche said: 'I tell you frankly that *I consider yours the greatest musical talent in Russia to-day.* Stronger and more original than Balakirev, loftier and more creative than Serov, incomparably more cultured than Rimsky-Korsakov' (who, after all, was not yet twenty-two, had had *no* musical education, and had produced nothing but that one symphony). '*In you I see the greatest—or rather the only—hope of our musical future!* You know quite well I'm not a flatterer; I never hesitated for a moment to tell you that your *Romans in the Coliseum* was a wretched piece of triviality and your *Storm* a museum of anti-musical curiosities.

Besides—everything you've done so far, the *Characteristic Dances* and the scene from *Boris Godunov* [1] not excepted, is in my opinion only preparatory, experimental school-work. Your own real creations may not appear for five years or so. But these ripe and classic works will surpass everything we have had since Glinka'.

[1] Nothing whatever is known of Tchaïkovsky's *Romans in the Coliseum*; the 'scene from *Boris Godunov*' was a setting of the love-scene between Marina and the Pretender at the fountain, which has unfortunately never been published.

CHAPTER II

1866–71

Overture in F major – homesickness – composition of First Symphony – nervous breakdown – *Danish Overture* – work on *The Voevoda* – 'longing for quiet existence' – the Symphony performed – Tchaïkovsky's attitude to the Balakirev group – début as a critic – friendship with the Shilovskys – visit to Paris – *Fatum* – the Desirée Artôt episode – performance of *The Voevoda* – Balakirev and *Fatum* – *Undine* – Russian folk-song arrangements – *Romeo and Juliet* – the abortive *Mandragora* – begins *The Oprichnik* – rejection of *Undine* – in Western Europe with Vladimir Shilovsky – new version of *Romeo and Juliet*.

TCHAÏKOVSKY arrived in Moscow still depressed by the fate of his cantata and at leaving the twins; lonely; and more than a little homesick. But he was greeted with warmth and kindness by at least two of the strangers he had come to live among. One of Laroche's friends, N. D. Kashkin, likewise a professor at the new Conservatoire, afterwards a critic, took to Tchaïkovsky at once. While Nicholas Rubinstein, an uncompromising idealist who concealed an extremely forceful personality under an air of aristocratic languor, but 'a very good and sympathetic man' with 'none of his brother's unapproachableness' (as Tchaïkovsky told the twins), overpowered the fledgeling professor with kindness. He not only insisted on taking him into his own house (which at first had to serve also as the Conservatoire building) but 'looked after him as if he were his nurse', lending him a dress-coat, forcing on him a present of half a dozen shirts, taking him to a tailor to be measured for a frock-coat—all within a week or two of his arrival. Yet, as a composer, Tchaïkovsky's Moscow life began as unhappily as his Petersburg life had ended. Immediately on his arrival he had begun the orchestration of the C minor Overture written at Kamenka the previous summer; the work helped him to kill his melancholy. But when it was finished Nicholas Rubinstein condemned it. The score was sent to Anton with no better result and the work had to wait till 1931—thirty-eight years after the composer's death—for its first performance.[1] Tchaïkovsky himself afterwards admitted that it was 'awful rubbish', but he used some of its material again in the first act of his opera *The Voevoda*. He appears to have made up his mind to write an opera on this subject, another of Ostrovsky's dramas, within a few weeks of his arrival in Moscow and at first decided to prepare his own libretto. But a year or more passed before anything was done. In the meantime he busied himself with the rescoring of his F major Overture, with which he made a very successful public début in Moscow at the end of March. Nicholas Rubinstein conducted.

Early in February he was able to write to Alexandra that he was 'gradually beginning to get used to Moscow, though loneliness often makes me miserable. My classes are very successful, to my

---

[1] The score was found among S. I. Taneev's papers in 1922 and has since been published.

great surprise; my nervousness has completely
vanished and I'm gradually acquiring the proper
professional air. My homesickness is also wearing
off, but Moscow is still a strange town for me,
and it will be a long time yet before I shall be
able to think without dread of having to stay here
for long years, perhaps for ever'. Still, his life
was by no means unrelievedly gloomy. He could
laugh heartily over *Pickwick*; his nerves were
steady; and he was having his leg pulled a good
deal about a pretty girl at a friend's house. And
at Easter he was able to spend a few days in
St. Petersburg.

In March Tchaïkovsky began his First Symphony. Though not programme-music, it was
given a title, *Winter Daydreams*, and the first two
movements had sub-titles. The composition
worried him excessively, for the fate of his cantata
and the C minor Overture had shaken his faith
in his own powers. He began to suffer from
insomnia and 'throbbing sensations in the head';
his nerves were completely upset; and he was
haunted by a conviction that he was destined to
die and leave the Symphony unfinished. Working feverishly far into the night in an attempt to
outwit destiny, he naturally made matters worse.
To crown everything he was disappointed of
another summer at Kamenka, owing to the state
of the roads, and obliged to console himself with
a holiday at Myatlev, near Petersburg. At the
end of June he had a very serious nervous
breakdown, suffering from hallucinations and

'an inescapeable sense of horror', indeed, was dangerously near the border-line of insanity. Nevertheless, he recovered sufficiently to return to Moscow by the end of August.

In Petersburg he had shown his unfinished Symphony to Anton Rubinstein and Zaremba, who had promptly condemned it. But in Moscow brighter prospects were opening up. The Conservatoire was flourishing. Not only was it to be housed in a building of its own—though not the present Conservatoire building—and the staff increased, but Nicholas Rubinstein had been able to double Tchaïkovsky's salary. After the banquet which followed the official opening of the new building on September 1st/13th, Tchaïkovsky, 'feeling', says Kashkin, 'that the first music to be heard in the new Conservatoire should be Glinka's, went to the piano and played the *Ruslan* Overture from memory'. The next month he composed a *Festival Overture on the Danish National Anthem* in celebration of the visit to Moscow of the Tsarevich with his bride, the Danish Princess Dagmar. (It is amusing to learn that the composer promptly sold the jewelled cuff-links with which the Tsarevich acknowledged the musical compliment, to one of his colleagues, the pianist, A. I. Dubuque.) By November the Symphony was finished and the scherzo played in Moscow almost immediately; and the adagio and scherzo were given in Petersburg at a Russian Music Society concert on February 11th/23rd, 1867. Anton Rubinstein had refused to play the whole of the Symphony, and the reception of these excerpts in both Moscow and Petersburg was distinctly cool. However, the two movements were almost the last things Anton Rubinstein conducted for the Society. Shortly afterwards he resigned from both the Society and the Conservatoire, being succeeded at the latter by Zaremba and as conductor by Balakirev.

During the winter Tchaïkovsky made the acquaintance of Ostrovsky, whom he so much admired. The dramatist, who lived in Moscow, agreed to help him with the libretto of *The Voevoda* and did actually give him the libretto of the first act in the spring of 1867. But, the composer having lost the manuscript, Ostrovsky had to rewrite it from memory and then seems to have lost patience, with the result that nearly the whole of the libretto was ultimately Tchaïkovsky's own. But the composition of the music must have gone very smoothly, for the score was finished by the end of the year. Foiled through lack of funds in an attempt to spend a holiday in Finland, Tchaïkovsky and Anatol spent the summer at Hapsal with the Davïdov ladies, pleasant weeks which the composer commemorated in a set of three piano pieces (one of them the popular *Chant sans Paroles*) entitled *Souvenir de Hapsal*, Op. 2, dedicated to Vera Davïdova. Already he talked happily of being 'weary of life', though he wished to escape from it not into extinction but into vegetation. 'In those moments when I am too lazy not only to talk but even to think', he writes to Alexandra, '*I long for a quiet, heavenly, happy existence,* and I can't imagine such an existence except in your immediate neighbourhood. You may be sure that one of these days you will have to devote part of your maternal care to your tired old brother. Perhaps you may think such a frame of mind leads to thoughts of marriage. No . . . my weariness has made me *too lazy* . . . to take upon myself the responsibility of a wife and children. Marriage is out of the question for me'. Yet when he went back to Moscow he felt no distaste for the pleasures of social life. His letters speak of 'coming home slightly drunk'[1]; 'spending two evenings running at the English Club' (the most fashionable and dissipated club in Moscow, where Nicholas Rubinstein spent night after night, playing for high stakes) and regretting that he cannot afford to become a member; 'coming home late with an overloaded stomach five days running'. In December, Laroche joined the staff of the Moscow Conservatoire and perhaps exercised a steadying influence on Tchaïkovsky.

That winter brought a definite increase to Tchaïkovsky's reputation. Nicholas Rubinstein played the dances from *The Voevoda* in December and the whole of the G minor Symphony, which was dedicated to him, for the first time on February

[1] His diary in later years has an endless succession of entries tersely recording: 'Drunkenness'. But this nightly brandy-drinking in solitude, which seems to have begun only after his disastrous marriage, was a very different matter from ordinary social drinking, which at some periods of his life he seems to have disliked.

3rd/15th, 1868, both with great success. Sixteen days later Tchaïkovsky made a rather disastrous first appearance as a conductor, directing his *Voevoda* dances at a charity concert in such a state of utter demoralization that the players were obliged simply to ignore his beat. He told Kashkin that he had had a recurrence of his former strange illusion that his head would fall off unless he held on to it tightly, a sensation which would certainly account for occasional lapses of attention. Laroche vividly recollected years afterwards how the unhappy composer had stood 'with the baton in his right hand, while his left firmly supported his fair beard'. Tchaïkovsky was so terrified that he made no attempt to conduct again for nearly ten years. Yet in another respect this charity concert had important consequences, for it assisted indirectly in Tchaïkovsky's *rapprochement* with the group of 'Petersburg amateurs', the celebrated 'mighty handful' of the Balakirev circle (Borodin, Rimsky-Korsakov, Mussorgsky and Cui), of which under slightly different circumstances he might so easily have become a member.

In his student days in Petersburg, Tchaïkovsky had known no musical people socially. Under Zaremba's wing he had been shepherded into the new Conservatoire and, but for the passing acquaintance with Serov, had met no musicians outside Conservatoire circles. The Conservatoire, staffed entirely by teachers of foreign blood, had given him a sound education, a hearty contempt for those who had *not* had a sound education, and a warm dislike of people who were constantly attacking 'Germans' and 'Jews'. His idol was a Jew and his bosom friend a German-Russian. Added to this he was always quick to suspect hostility to his own work even where none existed, and Cui, the journalistic mouthpiece of the 'handful', had dismissed his leaving cantata with contemptuous sarcasm. It is not unnatural that although he had never met any of the 'handful', he regarded them as a hostile group, while, according to Rimsky-Korsakov, they on their side considered him 'a mere child of the Conservatoire'.. Yet whereas his own loved and respected teacher, when conductor of the R.M.S. concerts, had repeatedly refused to play his music, the 'hostile' Balakirev in his very first season had written asking to see the score of the *Voevoda* dances. At first Tchaïkovsky was—characteristically—so suspicious of his good intentions that he actually refused to send it without a formal request signed by all the directors of the Society. Having received this, in January, 1868, he had sent off the *Dances* to Petersburg with a humble request for 'a word of encouragement'. 'It would be extremely gratifying to receive such from you'. Then at the already mentioned charity concert in February, Rimsky-Korsakov's *Serbian Fantasia* was played for the second time that winter in Moscow and dismissed as 'colourless and impersonal' by the critic of *The Entr'acte* (who praised Tchaïkovsky's *Dances*). This judgement provoked Tchaïkovsky, who had liked the *Fantasia*,

into making his début as a musical critic. In
another Moscow paper he put the *Entr'acte* critic
very firmly in his place, warmly praised the
Fantasia and referred flatteringly to Rimsky-
Korsakov's Symphony and his talent in general.
And on February 21st/March 4th, Balakirev
belatedly acknowledged the receipt of the *Voevoda*
dances, regretting that it was now too late to play
them that season. 'As for the word of encouragement . . . encouragement is suitable only for the
little children of art, whereas your score shows
me that you are a mature artist worthy of *severe
criticism.* When we meet, I shall be very glad to
give you my opinion; but it would be impossible
in a letter, for the letter would grow into a whole
essay—and from my unskilled pen that would be
deadly. It would be far better to play through
the piece together at the piano and criticize it bar
by bar'. Tchaïkovsky made no comment on this,
but a lively correspondence sprang up as to the
possibility of Nicholas Rubinstein's playing at a
Petersburg Free School concert for Balakirev.

When Tchaïkovsky visited Petersburg for a few
days in the spring he naturally called on Balakirev
and met the other members of his circle. 'He
showed himself to be a pleasant companion, with
a sympathetic personality', says Rimsky-Korsakov.
'His manner was simple and natural and he always
appeared to speak with warmth and sincerity.
On the first evening of our acquaintance Balakirev
got him to play the first movement of his G minor
Symphony, which pleased us very much. Our

former opinion of him changed to a more favourable one, though his Conservatoire education still
placed a considerable barrier between him and
us'. This favourable impression was mutual,
though Tchaïkovsky was drawn more particularly
to Rimsky-Korsakov, whom he soon began to call
by his nickname 'Korsinka', rather than to the
other members of what he called 'the Jacobin
Club'.

Another indirect link with the 'handful' had
been forged the previous year in a rather curious
way. Begichev, the Intendant of the Imperial
Theatres in Moscow, an elderly Don Juan, had
'adopted' (and afterwards married) a lady with a
past as colourful as his own: Marya Shilovskaya,
a former pupil of Dargomïzhsky and a friend of
Mussorgsky. Of her two sons by her first husband,
who died in 1870, one (Constantine) became
Tchaïkovsky's librettist, the other (Vladimir) a
favourite pupil and beloved friend. Vladimir
Shilovsky was consumptive, and in the summer of
1868 Begichev took the lad to Paris to consult
a specialist. Tchaïkovsky accompanied them
and completed the scoring of *The Voevoda* in
Paris.

Returning to Moscow in September, he began
the composition of a symphonic fantasia, *Fatum*,
and completed the rough sketch by the end of
October. In the meantime choral rehearsals of
The Voevoda had begun at the Bolshoy Theatre.
But a third-rate Italian opera company, run by
a certain Merelli, happened to be visiting Moscow

and drawing crowded houses, chiefly owing to
the superb art of the leading soprano, Désirée
Artôt. The opera chorus and orchestra were so
much occupied by their work with the Italians
that Tchaïkovsky, seeing that his own work was
going to be very perfunctorily prepared, asked
that the production should be postponed till the
visitors had gone. But before the Italians left,
they—or at least one of their number—had done
him still further injury.

Désirée Artôt, a pupil of Pauline Viardot-Garcia
and a lady five years older than Tchaïkovsky, has
the distinction of being the only woman who is
known to have made any impression on him,
other than a Platonic one. The progress of the
affair may be traced from Tchaïkovsky's letters to
Modest and Anatol during the period September/
November: 'Artôt is a charming creature; she
and I are good friends'. 'I am very busy writing
choruses and recitatives to Auber's *Domino Noir*
for Artôt's benefit'. 'I've become very friendly
with Artôt and she seems to like me. I've seldom
met such a nice, good, sensible woman'. 'I've
not written to you for a long time, but various
circumstances have made it impossible for me to
write letters, for all my leisure has been devoted
to a being of whom I am very fond'. He dedicates
a piano piece to her (the *Romance*, Op. 5) and on
Boxing Day/January 7th, 1869, announces to his
father his intention of marrying Désirée next
summer 'if nothing happens to prevent it'. At
the same time there are all sorts of obstacles:

Désirée's mother is against the match; Nicholas
Rubinstein and his other friends are doing their
best to stop it, lest it should interfere with his
career as a composer and reduce him to the rôle
of 'prima donna's husband'; the ardent lover
himself 'doesn't want to sacrifice his future to
her. . . . On the one hand I love her with all my
heart and soul, and feel I can't live any longer
without her; on the other, calm reason bids me
stop and think'. He would like his father's views
on the matter—and Ilya, like the old Micawber
he was, replied in a bless-you-my-children strain.
And the next we hear is in the course of a letter
to Anatol only a few weeks later: 'At the moment
I'm in a great state of excitement. *The Voevoda*
is going to be performed. Everyone is taking the
greatest pains', etc. etc. 'I've already begun
another opera . . . but I want to keep it a secret
for a while. How surprised people will be to find
half the opera already done in the summer', and
so on. And only then: 'As for the love-affair
. . . it's very doubtful whether I shall enter
Hymen's kingdom. Things are beginning to go
rather awry. I'll tell you more about it later.
No time now'. As a matter of fact, Désirée was
already betrothed to the Spanish baritone Padilla-
y-Ramos, whom she married the following
September. But although her brief return to
Moscow later in 1869 caused Tchaïkovsky some
painful hours, considering his sufferings from much
less important troubles he seems to have borne
his amorous disappointment extraordinarily well.

Indeed, Kashkin hints that his friend was in love with the artist rather than the woman, and says that the initiative in the affair was taken by Artôt.

The Voevoda had its first performance on January 30th/February 11th, 1869, and scored an apparent triumph, the composer receiving no less than fifteen calls. Yet the opera was repeated only four times more; Laroche criticized it adversely, thereby causing a quarrel which lasted for some months; and a few years later Tchaïkovsky himself destroyed the score, having used the best of the music in other works. (The *Dances*, however, had already been published separately as Op. 3, and sixty years or so later the whole opera was almost entirely reconstructed from existing parts by S. Popov.) On February 25th/March 9th Nicholas Rubinstein also played *Fatum* (another work destroyed in the seventies but posthumously reconstructed and published as Op. 77) at a Moscow R.M.S. concert. Tchaïkovsky immediately sent the score to Balakirev with a request that he would accept the dedication if he liked the piece. Balakirev accepted the dedication, almost without looking at the score, which had been borrowed first by Rimsky-Korsakov and then by Borodin. 'But in any case, whether I like it or not, I'll play it at the next concert', he assured the composer. He was as good as his word. *Fatum* was performed at a Petersburg R.M.S. concert on March 17th/29th, but Balakirev did *not* like it. In some embarrass-

ment he tried to write to Tchaïkovsky about it,
but the letter 'grew into a whole essay' and was
never sent. The letter he did send after a fortnight or so was quite frank enough, however:
'Your *Fatum* has been played. . . . There was
little applause, which I ascribe to the hideous din
at the end. . . .' But finally, after a good deal
of typically Balakirevian advice: 'I write with
perfect candour, feeling quite sure that you won't
change your intention of dedicating *Fatum* to me.
Your dedication is precious as a sign of your
sympathy—and I have a soft corner in my heart
for you'. To which Tchaïkovsky replied on May
3rd/15th: 'It was very wrong of me not to write
before and, by my silence, perhaps to give you
reason to think I had taken offence at your letter
criticizing *Fatum*. In the depths of my heart I
quite agree with your remarks about this concoc-
tion, though I admit I should have been very
happy if you could have found something to praise
in it—if only a little. Your letter is all fault-
finding—though quite justifiably. I admit I was
not delighted with your criticism, but I wasn't in
the least offended. I paid homage to the sincere
straightforwardness which is one of the most
delightful traits of your musical personality. Of
course I shan't withdraw the dedication, but I
hope somewhen to write something better for
you'. And he goes on to express the intense
indignation he and Nicholas Rubinstein were
feeling at the treatment Balakirev had received
from the Grand Duchess Helena Pavlovna, treat-

ment which resulted in his leaving the Russian Music Society. Nor was this indignation expressed only in private; Tchaïkovsky wrote a very outspoken article on the subject for the *Sovremennaya Letopis*. At the end of the letter he tells Balakirev: 'I am now occupied with the instrumentation of my opera *Undine*; one act is already finished; the other two will be scored in the summer'.

This *Undine*, to a Russian version of a French libretto based on Fouqué's celebrated tale, was the 'secret' opera that Tchaïkovsky had mentioned to Anatol in January. It was duly completed at Kamenka in July, and Begichev took the score to Petersburg. But there the composer was doomed to disappointment. Gedeonov, the Director of the Imperial Theatres, already had two new operas—by nonentities—on his hands and Tchaïkovsky was informed that *Undine* could not be produced that season. In the meantime he concluded a commission from Jurgenson: the arrangement of fifty Russian folk-songs for piano duet. He had done the first twenty-five during the autumn of 1868, taking the melodies from Villebois's collection—and altering them according to his fancy. Now, with Balakirev's permission, he took the second batch from the latter's collection, treating them a little more respectfully and winning the other's approval for at least a few of his arrangements. Of the whole fifty, only one had been collected by himself: a lovely melody he had heard sung (to ribald words) that summer at Kamenka, by a carpenter working outside the room in which he was orchestrating *Undine*. This set of folk-songs was only one of a considerable number of pot-boilers done for Jurgenson at this period under either Tchaïkovsky's own name or the pseudonym 'H. Cramer': piano arrangements of other people's works and even pot-pourris on his own *Voevoda* and Meyerbeer's *Pardon de Ploërmel*.

Balakirev appeared in Moscow in August, perhaps hoping that Nicholas Rubinstein would be able to help him in some way. 'I confess', wrote Tchaïkovsky, 'that his presence weighs on me', as indeed it had begun to weigh on Mussorgsky and Rimsky-Korsakov. 'He expects me to spend the whole day with him, and that bores me. He is a very good fellow and very well disposed toward me but—I don't know why—I can never feel absolutely at home with him. I particularly dislike the onesidedness of his musical opinions and the acerbity of his tone'. Nevertheless, it was during this visit that Balakirev induced Tchaïkovsky to write a concert-overture on the subject of *Romeo and Juliet*. For a month or so Tchaïkovsky was empty of ideas and Balakirev eagerly sketched out a beginning, of which Tchaïkovsky made no use. Towards the end of October, however, he was able to report that 'my overture is going ahead fairly quickly; already the greater part is fully sketched out and if nothing hinders me I hope it will be ready in a month and a half'. A fortnight later he sent Balakirev the

chief themes—and the dedication of what he hoped
was the promised 'something better'. Balakirev
was delighted with the *cor anglais* love-theme, but
critical of other points. When he and Rimsky-
Korsakov visited Moscow in January, Tchaïkovsky
'of course, saw them every day. Balakirev is beginning to admire me more and more; Korsakov
has dedicated a very good song to me. They are
both pleased with my overture'. In fact at this
period Tchaïkovsky was, so far as his residence in
Moscow permitted, a member of the 'Balakirev
circle'. [1]

With *Undine* still unproduced, Tchaïkovsky was
already thinking of a third opera. In January,
1870, he began one on a fantastic subject,
Mandragora, and wrote one number, a 'Chorus
of Flowers and Insects' (afterwards sung at an
R.M.S. concert as a 'Chorus of Elves'), but
abandoned the work in consequence of Kashkin's
criticism. He turned instead to Lazhechnikov's
tragedy, *The Oprichnik*, but for a time that also
stuck at the first chorus, which he had simply
lifted, words and all, from *The Voevoda*. The
failure first of *Romeo and Juliet* on March 4th/16th
and then, a fortnight later, of five excerpts from
the first act of *Undine*, only confirmed him in his
conviction that 'nobody takes any interest in what
I write' and discouraged him from working at
The Oprichnik. He 'yearned so for sympathy and

---

[1] Simultaneously with *Romeo and Juliet*—in November/
December, 1869—Tchaïkovsky wrote his first songs, the half-
dozen which make up Op. 6.

appreciation', and the only encouraging word came from the 'handful'. 'At our meetings we keep on playing the score of *Romeo* that you sent us', wrote Balakirev, 'and we are all delighted with a great deal of it. Stassov (Vlad.) is extraordinarily pleased and says our army has now been reinforced'. Balakirev insisted on despotically supervising the work of the recruit, as of the rest of his forces; but far from resenting his advice as to the improvement of parts of *Romeo*, Tchaïkovsky acted on it and largely rewrote the work on the lines suggested, during the summer in Switzerland. In the meantime he had suffered a fresh disappointment. In the middle of May the Opera Committee—which nine months later was to reject Mussorgsky's *Boris*—turned down *Undine*. Four or five years later Tchaïkovsky himself destroyed the score, after using some of the numbers in other works, but at the time he felt himself to be the victim of terrible injustice. He left Petersburg to join Vladimir Shilovsky in Paris with a heart full of bitterness.

Shilovsky was very ill, but Tchaïkovsky got him away from Paris to Bad Soden, near Frankfurt-am-Main, in June. 'We lead a monotonous existence and get very bored', he wrote to Modest, 'but for that very reason my health is excellent. . . . I'm very lazy and haven't the slightest wish to work'. At the Beethoven Centenary Festival at Mannheim, he heard the D major Mass for the first time and thought it 'a creation of the highest genius'. (But Tchaïkovsky always re-

spected Beethoven a great deal more than he
loved him.) At Wiesbaden he found Nicholas
Rubinstein 'in the act of losing his last ruble at
roulette . . . but firmly convinced that he's going
to break the bank before he leaves'. The out-
break of the Franco-German War in July sent
them all scuttling over the frontier into Switzerland, to escape the expected French invasion, and
after six weeks at Interlaken, where his 'astonish-
ment and admiration in the presence of these
sublime beauties of Nature passed all bounds',
Tchaïkovsky wandered back to Moscow by way
of Munich, Vienna and Petersburg.

Having orchestrated the new version of *Romeo
and Juliet*, which was published in Berlin by Bote
and Bock the following year, he resumed work on
The Oprichnik. But he was disappointed of a
Petersburg performance of *Romeo*, since, owing to
financial difficulties, the Free School was unable
to give any concerts that winter. 'I so badly
want to hear my overture under your direction',
he had written to Balakirev, 'that I would come
to Petersburg—though for one day only. Of
course, this expedition must remain a secret
between you and me, for it's really ludicrous to
go four hundred miles to hear one's own things!'
Two or three years later he wrote to the publisher
Bessel in exactly the same strain: 'I tell you quite
as a secret that I'd like to be present at the first
symphony concert in Petersburg, so as to hear my
Symphony. As I don't on any account want
people to know about this, I must ask you to give

me your word of honour not to betray me. . . .
For heaven's sake, not a word, or my whole joke
will be turned into a terrible piece of unpleasant-
ness'. And there were other occasions when
Tchaïkovsky attended performances of his own
works in this furtive way.

CHAPTER III

1871–77

EARLY in 1871 Tchaïkovsky, hoping to raise a little money, decided to give a concert. The desire to arouse interest by a new work of his own, combined with lack of funds to engage an orchestra, more or less obliged him to write a string quartet—in spite of his lack of interest in chamber music—and the Quartet in D, Op. 11, was the result. For the chief theme of the slow movement, the famous *andante cantabile*, Tchaïkovsky took the folk-song he had heard at his sister's in the summer of 1869. But the Quartet, written rather hurriedly in February and played at the concert on March 16th/28th, was only an interlude in the composition of *The Oprichnik*. The period as a whole was a rather disturbed one. In the summer Tchaïkovsky made quite a round of visits—to his elder brother, to Anatol in Kiev,

to Kamenka, to the home of a friend (N. D.
Kondratyev) at Nizy in the Ukraine (where he
finished his text-book on harmony), and to
Vladimir Shilovsky at Ussovo. (Perhaps it was
during this visit that Shilovsky was invited or
allowed to compose and orchestrate one of the
entr'actes in *The Oprichnik*.) On returning to
Moscow he at last managed to break away from
Nicholas Rubinstein's too hospitable roof. Rubinstein was the exact counterpart of Balakirev in
well-meaning despotism as in other respects, and
he had insisted on having Tchaïkovsky's company
constantly and in arranging every detail of his life
for him—to all of which Tchaïkovsky had meekly,
though unwillingly, submitted. But he now took
a three-roomed flat of his own and engaged a
man-servant. From about the same time dates the
beginning of his more or less regular work as one
of the musical critics of the *Russky Vedomosti*, which
continued till 1876. Laroche having returned to
Petersburg, his post as critic was nominally filled
by N. A. Hubert, but the work was actually
shared by Hubert, Tchaïkovsky and Kashkin.

In the autumn the correspondence with Bala-
kirev was as lively as ever. And now there are
references to other members of the circle, besides
Tchaïkovsky's favourite 'Korsinka'. 'Make
Borodin hurry up and finish his splendid sym-
phony' (i.e. the B minor), he writes to Balakirev.
While Balakirev is '*very* anxious to perform your
D major chorus' (the 'Chorus of Flowers and
Insects'), and shortly afterwards sends a detailed

plan for converting this solitary chorus into a
'lyrical and descriptive' cantata, *Night*, with 'an
instrumental scherzo in the style of *Queen Mab*,
depicting the hum of gnats, etc.', fantastic
choruses of spirits, and an orchestral epilogue
depicting dawn and sunrise. To which Tchaïkovsky replies: 'I like your idea for a cantata,
Night, very much and shall certainly make use
of it, though not in the immediate future. At the
moment I am employing all my few free hours on
my *opera*, *The Oprichnik*, which I am very anxious
to finish during the present winter. I dare say
this unlucky opera will share the fate of my
Undine, but none the less I want to finish it, so
I can't begin another composition yet for a while'.
He is also very anxious to know at which Free
School concert his chorus will be given. 'Who
knows whether I may not manage to skip over
to "Peter"?' Balakirev replies that it will be
done on December 18th/30th, and 'we shall all
be very glad to see you'.

But before that date Tchaïkovsky had left
Russia and was on his way to Nice. The episode
is curious and not easily explicable, considering
his anxiety to finish *The Oprichnik*. 'I must tell
you that at Shilovsky's urgent desire I am going
abroad for a month', he writes to Anatol on
December 2nd/14th. 'I shall start in a week or
two. But as no one in Moscow—except Rubinstein—must know anything about it, they must all
be made to think I've gone to Sasha's', i.e. to
Kamenka. After a month at Nice, where even

the 'many pleasant hours' were shot through with
melancholy—'I have grown old and can enjoy
nothing more. I live on my memories and hopes.
But what is there to hope for?'—he returned to
Moscow, worked during February and March at
a Festival Cantata commissioned for a forthcoming Polytechnic Exhibition, and completed
The Oprichnik by the beginning of May.

In the meantime Balakirev had, in an ecstasy
of religious mania, disappeared from the world of
music, and nine years were to elapse before they
resumed contact. It is idle to conjecture how
Tchaïkovsky would have developed if he had
stayed under Balakirev's influence, but it is interesting to note that he remained an ally of the
'mighty handful' until the 'handful' itself began
to disintegrate. As we shall see, the link was not
immediately broken—though weakened—by Balakirev's disappearance. Tchaïkovsky was never
more completely a nationalist than in *The
Oprichnik* and the work he wrote during the
summer of 1872: the Second Symphony, with its
first and last movements based on folk-songs.
(The second, a march, was taken from the ill-fated
Undine.) The Symphony was begun at Kamenka
in June, continued at Nizy and Ussovo, and
orchestrated in the autumn after the composer's
return to Moscow.

Tchaïkovsky's letters that winter are full of
familiar refrains: 'Nothing particular happens
to any of us. . . . We go to the Conservatoire as
usual; sometimes we meet in the old way for a

general "booze"; and are just as bored as last
year. Boredom consumes us all, and the reason
is that we are growing old. Yes . . . every
moment brings us nearer the grave. . . . As for
myself, I have only one interest in life: my success
as a composer'. His sight was giving him trouble
and as usual his nerves were bad, 'often getting
out of order for no obvious reason'. He was also
worrying about 'the not very consoling fate of my
compositions. The Symphony, on which I build
great hopes, will probably not be performed before
the middle of January at the earliest'. However,
at Christmas the even greater worry as to the
fate of *The Oprichnik* was removed. Tchaïkovsky
was summoned to Petersburg and the Opera
Committee accepted the work unanimously.

During this visit to Petersburg the remaining
members of the 'handful', with the important
exception of Mussorgsky, expressed their delight
with the Second Symphony, particularly the
finale [1]; Rimsky-Korsakov's wife undertook the
piano-duet arrangement of the Symphony; while
even Balakirev made a single, fleeting appearance
specially to hear Tchaïkovsky's String Quartet.
And before leaving Petersburg, Tchaïkovsky asked
Stassov to suggest a subject for a symphonic
fantasia. Stassov suggested three—Shakespeare's

[1] Cui attacked the Second Symphony when it was played
in Petersburg. And he attacked *The Oprichnik*, comparing it
unfavourably with *Boris*. But he had also handled *Boris* very
roughly. Cui's critical method was peculiar to himself. Having
belaboured his antagonists with tremendous enthusiasm, he
would turn round and knock down a few of his friends just to
show that he was quite impartial.

Tempest, Ivanhoe, or Gogol's *Taras Bulba*—giving him a detailed programme for *The Tempest* which the composer accepted in every detail, dedicating the resultant work to the critic.

The Second Symphony was played in Moscow on January 26th/February 7th, 1873, with such success that it was repeated at another concert the same season. Then Tchaïkovsky was commissioned to write incidental music for the production in May of Ostrovsky's poetic play, *Snow Maiden,* work which he completed rather hurriedly during the spring, patching in bits of odd material from *Undine.* He again spent the summer abroad, returning to Russia early in August to spend a couple of weeks with Shilovsky at Ussovo. Shilovsky had to go to Moscow for a short time, and, for the first time in his life, Tchaïkovsky found himself alone in the heart of the Russian countryside. Years afterwards he described the peculiar delights of those few days: 'I found myself in a mood of serene exaltation, wandered in the day through the woods, walked each evening in the deep valley, and at night, sitting by the open window, listened to the solemn silence all around, broken now and again by some indefinite sound of nature. During those two weeks, without the least labour—just as if I had been guided by some supernatural power—I sketched out my *Tempest*'. The piece so fluently written, actually in ten days, was orchestrated in the autumn and given its first performance in Moscow on December 7th/19th. There was again

a triumph. And a second String Quartet, in F
major, Op. 22, written early in 1874, scored an
immediate success.

The tide of Tchaïkovsky's fortune seemed to
have definitely turned. He had been moaning
to the publisher Bessel in October: 'It's useless
for you to hope that *The Oprichnik* will be put on
next season. It will never be given at all, simply
because I'm not known personally to the "great
ones" of this world in general and to those of the
Petersburg Opera in particular. Isn't it perfectly
absurd that Kondratyev [1] should have chosen
Mussorgsky's *Boris Godunov* for his benefit, although
it's been rejected by the Committee? And
Platonova also is interested in this work, while no
one wants to know anything about my opera,
which has been accepted'. But almost immediately news came that *The Oprichnik* was to be
produced in the spring of 1874. Like every
other Russian opera composer of the period,
Tchaïkovsky had to run the double gauntlet of
the Censorship (which cut the figure of Ivan the
Terrible out of the *dramatis personæ*) and of the
conductor Napravnik with his blue pencil. At
first he accepted all Napravnik's suggestions with
surprising humility, but as the rehearsals went on
—he stayed in Petersburg with his father while
they were in progress—he became more and more
annoyed by Napravnik's drastic surgery. To make
matters worse, he was a prey to self-dissatisfaction,

[1] G. P. Kondratyev, stage-manager of the Maryinsky Theatre.
Not to be confused with Tchaïkovsky's friend, N. D. Kondratyev
(whom he once likened to Major Pendennis).

disliking his work a little more at every rehearsal
and writing to his friends in Moscow that he
would prefer them not to come and hear it as
'*there's nothing good in the thing*'. At the same time,
he was careful enough to get tickets for them, and
one imagines he would have been rather badly
hurt if they had taken him at his word. Actually
the *première* (April 12th/24th) was attended by
Nicholas Rubinstein and almost the whole of
the Moscow Conservatoire staff. But even the
brilliant success of the first performance, followed by a supper at which the Petersburg and
Moscow branches of the Russian Music Society
combined to do him honour, did not end Tchaïkovsky's torment of dissatisfaction. Within three
days he fled to Italy and wandered from Venice
to Rome, from Rome to Naples, Naples to Florence, in utter wretchedness. Venice he found
'gloomy', Rome 'uninteresting'. 'At Naples it
came to such a pass that every day I shed tears
from sheer homesickness. . . . But the chief
source of all my misery remains in Petersburg.
The Oprichnik torments me'. Yet he had no
sooner returned to Petersburg in May than he
thought of a fresh opera, began it the next month,
and actually completed it, orchestration and all,
in the course of the summer.

The history of this work, *Vakula the Smith*, is
curious, that of its composer's behaviour in connexion with it still more so. Three or four years
before, Polonsky had been commissioned by the
Grand Duchess Helena Pavlovna to prepare for

Serov a libretto on Gogol's *Christmas Eve*. But
Serov having died with the work hardly begun,
the Grand Duchess had decided to offer two
prizes for the best settings of the libretto. In the
meantime she herself had died in 1873 and the
competition was now being run by the R.M.S.
The closing date was fixed for August 1st/13th,
1875; the first prize work would be performed
at the Maryinsky Theatre; but naturally no un-
successful setting of the libretto would stand any
chance of production. Considering that last fact,
it is understandable that Tchaïkovsky did not wish
to enter unless he was practically certain of winning. In itself there was nothing very despicable,
if not particularly creditable, in his preliminary manœuvres to discover whether Rimsky-
Korsakov, Anton Rubinstein, or even Balakirev
was competing. But this was only the first of a
series of incidents, impossible to explain away and
difficult to excuse, unless on the grounds that an
artist is justified in sticking at nothing in order to
succeed, and that Tchaïkovsky 'felt he might go
out of his mind if *Vakula* failed'. He had begun
his opera and completed it so hurriedly under
the impression that the competition closed in
August, *1874*. Now discovering that he was a
year too soon, and that he would have to wait all
that time before the fate of his work was decided,
he sounded Napravnik and G. P. Kondratyev as
to the possibility of having his *Vakula* produced
at once, regardless of the other competitors. He
naturally received a sharp rap over the knuckles

from Napravnik and the Grand Duke Constantine
Nikolaevich, the chairman of the jury, and wrote
expressing his regrets for his 'stupid mistake' and
repudiating 'ulterior motives'. But Tchaïkovsky's
indiscretions did not end there. Instead of
keeping the authorship secret, as he was in
honour bound to do by the terms of the competition, he had the overture publicly performed in
Moscow in November, 1874—and conducted by
Nicholas Rubinstein, *one of the judges.* Although
the score submitted had to be in a copyist's hand,
it bore a distinguishing motto in the composer's
own handwriting, well known to almost every
member of the jury. And just before the actual
judging, Tchaïkovsky sent Rimsky-Korsakov, one
of their number, a quite unnecessarily flattering
letter, in which he naïvely stresses his anxiety to
win. Indeed, the whole affair was scandalous in
the extreme. All Petersburg knew that Tchaïkovsky was the winner before the jury themselves
were supposed to have learned the names of the
competitors. Rimsky-Korsakov consoled himself
afterwards with the reflection that 'no harm was
done, since Tchaïkovsky's opera was undoubtedly
the best of those sent in'. But the affair was
hardly the less discreditable on that account.

In the meantime, Tchaïkovsky was busy with
a new composition, the famous B flat minor
Piano Concerto, written (not without considerable labour) during November and December,
1874, and orchestrated a month or so later. The
Concerto was a source of fresh pain to his morbidly

sensitive nature, for Nicholas Rubinstein, to whom
it was originally dedicated and for whom it had
been specially written, abused it roundly and,
according to the composer himself, with unnecessary brutality. 'Deeply offended . . . I left
the room in silence and went upstairs. I could
not have spoken a word for rage and agitation'.
He altered the dedication, offering it to Hans von
Bülow, whom he had never met but whom he
knew to be interested in his work, and it was years
before he completely forgave Nicholas Rubinstein.
At the same time Laroche had just been abusing
his *Tempest* after its performance in Petersburg.
True, the Stassov-Rimsky-Korsakov group were
writing him letters of sympathy and congratula-
tion, and even Cui had been moved to public
praise of *The Tempest* and the Second String
Quartet. But that did not satisfy his craving for
praise from his Moscow friends. In these moods
he felt that they were 'mere professional colleagues'. 'I have clear proofs that not one of
them gives me the tenderness and affection that
my spirit needs'. He already felt 'often drawn
towards a monastic life, or something of the kind.
. . . In my nature there is so much fear of
mankind, so much unnecessary timidity and
mistrust—in short, a host of characteristics which
make me more and more misanthropical. . . .
All through the winter I've been depressed,
so depressed that I've often been brought to
the verge of despair and obliged to long for
death'.

The summer—divided between Ussovo, Nizy and Verbovka, another property of the Davïdovs, near Kamenka — brought relief. Tchaïkovsky wrote his Third Symphony, 'commenced June 5th/17th at Ussovo, completed August 1st/13th, 1875, at Verbovka', as a note on the score records. And he began a ballet, *Swan Lake*, commissioned by the Imperial Theatres. The successful production of both the new Symphony and the Piano Concerto in Moscow in November, with the favourable result of the opera competition, dispelled his depression altogether, and he was in exceptionally high spirits during a visit to the West with Modest that winter. It was during this visit, in Paris, that he saw *Carmen* for the first time, with Célestine Galli-Marié in the title rôle. (He had already known the vocal score.) 'Peter Ilyich had never before been so completely carried away by any piece of modern music as by *Carmen*', says his brother. 'Bizet's death three months after the first performance still further strengthened his almost unhealthy passion for the opera. . . . I had never before seen Peter Ilyich so excited after a dramatic performance'. In Paris, also, the composer began his third and last String Quartet (E flat minor, Op. 30), dedicated to the memory of his colleague, the violinist Laub, who had died the previous March. But his chief preoccupation was the finding of a new opera subject, 'one concerned with real human beings, not lay-figures . . . in close touch with our life and time . . . a simple, realistic drama', as Modest says.

In short, something of the *Carmen* type.[1] 'I am
working at full steam to finish the Quartet', he
writes to Modest on February 10th/22nd, 1876,
after his return to Moscow. 'After that'—the
Quartet was performed about five weeks later—
'I shall rest for a while, i.e. do nothing but finish
my ballet'. (That also was done by the end of
March.) 'I shan't start on anything new till I've
decided on an opera. I'm still wavering between
Ephraim'—a libretto concocted by Vladimir Shilovsky's brother, Constantine, in imitation of *Aïda*—
'and *Francesca da Rimini*, but I think it's going to
be the latter'. It *was* the latter. Only, instead
of an opera, *Francesca* became an orchestral piece,
sketched roughly during the summer in Paris.

For in the summer Tchaïkovsky was again in
the West, first taking a cure at Vichy, then going
to Bayreuth in August for the famous first performance of the *Ring*, which he was to report for
the *Russky Vedomosti*. Among the other Russian
musicians present were Nicholas Rubinstein
(who shared rooms with Tchaïkovsky), Cui and
Laroche; he also made the acquaintance of Liszt,
'who received me with extraordinary kindness',
and called on Wagner, who apparently did not
receive him at all. As for the *Ring* itself, Tchaïkovsky was obviously confused and oppressed by
it all. He found the music of *Das Rheingold*
'incredible nonsense', though with 'delightful
moments'. There might be a lot of fine stuff in

---

[1] Again, only six months before his death, he advised Modest
to 'find or invent *a not fantastic* subject—something in the style
of *Carmen* or *Cavalleria Rusticana*'.

the *Ring* but it was all much too long-drawn. 'To be sure there are beautiful passages, but as a whole it's deadly boring. The ballet *Sylvia* is a thousand times finer'. 'After the last chords of *Götterdämmerung* I felt as if I'd been let out of prison'. 'Bayreuth has left me with a disagreeable memory', he wrote to Modest, 'although my artistic pride has been flattered more than once. It appeared that I'm by no means as unknown in the West as I'd supposed'. Tchaïkovsky never grew to like Wagner's music, except *Lohengrin*, which he thought by far his best work, and though his published reports from Bayreuth show that he tried to be fair to it—no mean virtue in a Russian critic of those days—his impressions are all curiously blurred. It was with profound relief that he escaped to Nuremberg and Vienna, and then made for the seclusion of Verbovka.

From Verbovka in August he announced to Modest a project which, when actually carried into effect, was to have the most disastrous consequences. 'I have now to surmount a very critical moment of my life. Later I will write you about it in more detail; in the meantime I will tell you only that *I've decided to marry*. That is irrevocable. . . .' And again, three weeks later, from Moscow: 'The result of my thinking is that from to-day onward I shall seriously try to enter into legal marriage with someone or other. I am aware that my *inclinations* are the greatest and most unconquerable obstacle to happiness, and I must struggle with my nature with all my

strength. . . . I shall do everything possible to
marry this year, and, even if my courage is in-
sufficient for that, I shall in any case break for
ever with my habits'. A week later still: 'How
delightful to come home in the evening to my
pleasant little room and settle down with a book!
At this moment I hate, probably not less than you
do, that beautiful unknown being who will force
me to change my way of living. Don't be afraid;
I shan't hurry in this matter'. On September
28th/October 10th: 'There are people who do
not despise me for my vices only because they
began to love me when they did not yet suspect
that I was actually a man with a lost reputation.
This is true, for instance, of Sasha [his sister]. I
know that she guesses *everything* and *forgives* everything. . . . You can imagine how terrible this is,
for people to blame me and forgive me, when actually
I am not to blame for anything! And isn't it an
appalling thought that people dear to me are
sometimes *ashamed* of me? But it has been so a
hundred times, and will be so a hundred times in
the future. In short, I should like to marry or
enter into an open liaison with some woman so
as to shut the mouths of contemptible gossipers,
whose opinion I do not value in the least but who
can hurt those near to me. . . . The carrying out
of my plans is by no means as near as you think.
I am so confirmed in my habits and tastes that it
is impossible to cast them off like an old glove.
Besides I am far from possessing an iron will and
since writing to you I have already given way

three times to my natural inclinations'. In October he reassured Sasha herself: 'Please don't worry about my marriage . . . which won't come off before next year. During the next few months I shall only look around and prepare myself a little for matrimony, which I consider necessary for various reasons. Rest assured that I shan't plunge heedlessly into the abyss of an unlucky union'. He told Kashkin that what he needed was not a mate but a companion and housekeeper. He was lonely and needed 'some elderly spinster or widow' who would 'understand' him, 'without any pretence of ardent passion'. In short, this marriage project was envisaged mainly as a disguise of his homosexuality rather than as an attempt to restore sexual normality.

It was during this period (October/November) that he wrote *Francesca da Rimini*, finishing the score on November 5th/17th. Nineteen days later *Vakula the Smith* was produced in Petersburg at the Maryinsky Theatre. This time Tchaïkovsky himself was satisfied with his work; even Cui assured him it was bound to be a brilliant success; but the public thought otherwise. In spite of the admirable production, *Vakula* was a failure, and immediately afterwards came news of the failure of *Romeo and Juliet* simultaneously in Vienna (under Richter) and Paris (under Pasdeloup).

A little balm to poor Tchaïkovsky's soul was provided by a meeting with Leo Tolstoy, whose novels he enthusiastically admired, but by whom he was unimpressed in the flesh. However,

Tolstoy, whose reactions to music were very naïve, wept at the *andante cantabile* of his D major Quartet, and—'I never felt so flattered in my life and so proud of my creative power as when L. Tolstoy, sitting beside me, listened to my *andante* while the tears streamed from his eyes'. But Tchaïkovsky seems to have met his trio of reverses with quite unusual buoyancy, a buoyancy reflected alike in the light-hearted *Rococo Variations* for 'cello and orchestra, in his eager badgering of Stassov to provide him with a scenario for an operatic *Othello*, and in an unusually playful letter to Modest (January 2nd/14th, 1877): 'Dear Mr. Modest Ilyich! I don't know whether you remember me, but I'm your own brother and Professor at the Moscow Conservatoire. I have also written several compositions: operas, symphonies, overtures, etc. Once upon a time you honoured me with your personal attention', and so on in the same vein. In February he actually plucked up courage to conduct his *Slavonic March* at the Moscow Opera House, apparently with sensations less alarming than in the old days, for he forthwith announced his intention of taking every opportunity to conduct, with a view to a foreign tour on which he would have to direct his own compositions. But he wisely left the first performance of *Francesca* a few days later in the safe hands of Nicholas Rubinstein.

CHAPTER IV

1877

CONSIDERING all it brought him—the real
beginning of the extraordinary connexion with
Nadezhda von Meck, the tragic marriage with its
so nearly fatal sequel, the composition of two of
his best works—the year 1877 might well be
considered the most important of Tchaïkovsky's
life. Certainly the note of subjective emotion,
which had hitherto been seldom if ever noticeable
in his music, became after this ever more and
more insistent, sharply differentiating his work
from that of all his Russian contemporaries.

Nadezhda von Meck was in 1877 a widow of
forty-six, cultured, much travelled, a lover of
music in general and of Tchaïkovsky's music in
particular. Her husband had died only the year
before, leaving her eleven children (of whom seven
were still living with her) and a very large fortune.
Eccentric as she was, her enormous wealth enabled
her to gratify the most extravagant of her
numerous whims. After her husband's death

she entirely shut herself up in her family circle. Tchaïkovsky himself never saw her except at a distance and they never exchanged a word of conversation. On one occasion when they met by accident both were overcome by confusion and passed on hurriedly. Although Tchaïkovsky's niece, Anna Davïdova, married Nadezhda's son Nicholas in 1884, the bride's parents never met the bridegroom's mother. Yet she gave Tchaïkovsky his financial independence and for fourteen years they carried on a constant, voluminous and extremely intimate correspondence, often dreadfully gushing on her side but (one feels) none the less sincere; profoundly revealing, if less perfectly sincere, on his. History records no stranger, more freakish friendship.

Already towards the end of 1876, through one of her house-musicians, the violinist Kotek, a friend and ex-pupil of Tchaïkovsky's, Nadezhda had commissioned him at an absurdly generous fee to arrange some of his smaller pieces for violin and piano. And the epistolary acquaintanceship thus begun ripened rapidly. On February 15th/27th she says she would like to tell him of her 'fantastic enthusiasm' for him, assuring him that it is 'ideal, abstract, lofty and noble'. 'You may call me a fool or a lunatic, but you must not laugh at me. All this would, perhaps, be ridiculous if it were not intended so seriously and sincerely'. Two or three weeks later, after asking for his photograph, she writes: 'In my opinion it is not personal intercourse which draws people together, but similarity of opinions, feelings and sympathies, so that one person may draw near to another, though (in a sense) a stranger. . . . All I have heard of you—both good and bad—gives me such extraordinary pleasure that I lay my warmest sympathy at your feet. I am happy at the thought that the man and the artist in you are so preciously and harmoniously united. There was a time when I was very anxious to make your personal acquaintance; but now the more you fascinate me the more I fear your acquaintanceship; I prefer to think of you from afar, to hear you speak in your music and to share your feelings through it'. Tchaïkovsky completely understood this 'fantastic feeling' of hers and reciprocated it, recognizing her as a kindred spirit in more respects than one. 'The circumstance that we both suffer from one and the same malady would alone bring us nearer to each other', he told her. 'This malady is misanthropy; but a quite peculiar form of misanthropy, for it does not spring from either hatred of or contempt for mankind. Those who suffer from this complaint do not fear the evils which their fellow-creatures may bring upon them, but they fear the disillusionment . . . which generally follows upon every intimacy. There was a time when I was so possessed by this fear of mankind that I became almost insane. . . . I had to fight it out with myself, and God alone knows what this conflict cost me! . . . Work saved me. . . . Those few successes which I have been allowed have given me consolation

and encouragement, so that the longings which
used often to drive me to hallucinations and
insanity have almost entirely lost their power over
me. . . . I'm not at all surprised that, in spite of
your love of my music, you don't wish to make my
acquaintance. You are afraid you will fail to find
in my personality all those qualities with which
your idealizing imagination has endowed me.
And in that you are quite right'. As for the
music itself: 'Whether I write well or ill—at any
rate, I write from inward necessity. I speak the
language of music because I always have something to say'.

As if to mock Tchaïkovsky's boast of conquered
'longings' and depression, they returned with
renewed force that spring. He was heavily in
debt but when, early in May, Mme. von Meck
wrote commissioning an original piece at a
ridiculous fee, he declined to accept the commission. It would have been a merely manufactured
piece and he declined to offer 'false coin in
exchange for true'. However, 'at the present
moment', he adds—this is on May 1st/13th, 'I am
completely absorbed in my symphony, which I
began in the winter', the Fourth Symphony.
'I should like to dedicate it to you, for I believe
you will find in it an echo of your most intimate
thoughts and feelings. . . . I am in a very
worried and irritable state of mind, unfavourable
to composition, which is all to the disadvantage
of the symphony'. A week later he wrote to
another friend: 'I am very much changed,

especially in mind, since we met last. . . . Life
is terribly empty, boring and trivial. I am
seriously considering matrimony as a lasting tie.
The only thing that remains unalterable is my
delight in composition. . . . But for my work at
the Conservatoire, which I dislike more and more
every year, I might perhaps be able to accomplish
something really valuable'.

Ten days later still, at the singer Lavrovskaya's,
'the conversation fell upon opera texts. . . .
Suddenly Lavrovskaya remarked, "What about
Eugene Onegin?" The idea struck me as wild
and I said nothing. Later, however, lunching
alone at a restaurant, I remembered *Onegin* . . .
and found the idea possible. . . . I soon made up
my mind, and set off at once in search of Pushkin's
works. . . . I was delighted when I read the poem.
I spent a sleepless night; result—the scenario of a
splendid opera on Pushkin's text. The very next
day I went to Constantine Shilovsky and he is
now working like the wind at my scenario'.
Tchaïkovsky completed the sketch of the Fourth
Symphony but postponed the orchestration till the
end of the summer, in order to concentrate on
Eugene Onegin. At the beginning of June, with an
extraordinary secret on his mind, he went to stay
at the Shilovskys' great house at Glebovo, where
Onegin went ahead rapidly. Tchaïkovsky was 'in
love with the image of Tatyana'—he was working
at the letter scene, with which he began the opera
—'under the spell of Pushkin's verse, and writing
the music under an irresistible compulsion. I am

quite buried in the composition of the opera'.
By June 23rd/July 5th two-thirds of the work was
sketched out.   But on that date he could keep his
secret no longer.

   He announced in a series of letters to his family
that he had been engaged for nearly a month and
proposed to get married, as secretly as possible,
in a week or two.   'Please don't worry about me',
he wrote to Anatol.   'I've thought it over well,
and I am taking this important step with a quiet
mind.   You will see that I really am calm when
I tell you that—with the prospect of marriage
before me—I have been able to write two-thirds
of my opera'.   (Ten days later he says he 'would
certainly have been able to do more, but for
my agitated state of mind'.)   'My bride is no
longer very young'—actually, twenty-eight—'but
otherwise suitable in every way. . . . She is poor
and her name is Antonina Ivanovna Milyukova'.
(In another letter he adds that 'she is rather
pretty, of spotless reputation . . . and moderate
education, but apparently good and capable of
loyal attachment'.)   'Ask Father not to say a
word about it to anyone'.   In a letter to
Nadezhda von Meck (July 3rd/15th) he gives a
more detailed account of how his engagement had
come about and quite a different impression of his
own attitude to the affair.   The girl, whom he
had met some time before at the Conservatoire
but remembered only vaguely, had sent him a
·love-letter, a letter 'so warmly and sincerely
written that I decided to answer it, which I had

always carefully avoided doing in previous cases
of the same kind. Without going into details, I
will tell you only . . . that I finally accepted my
future wife's invitation and visited her. Why did
I do that? It now seems to me that some
mysterious power drew me to this girl. When we
met, I repeated that for her love I could return
only sympathy and gratitude. But later I began
to consider how thoughtlessly I had acted. If
I didn't love her . . . why had I gone to see her,
and how would it all end? I saw that I had
gone too far and that if I now suddenly turned
from her, I should make her really unhappy and
drive her to a tragic end. I was faced with an
unpleasant alternative: either I must keep my
freedom at the cost of a human life, or I must
marry. There was nothing for it but to choose
the latter course. So one fine evening I went to
her, told her frankly that I couldn't love her, but
that I would be her faithful and grateful friend;
I described my character in detail, my irritability,
the unevenness of my temperament, my misanthropy—and my material position. Then I
asked her if she would be my wife. Her answer,
of course, was that she would. The fearful
torments I have suffered since that evening are
not to be described. Which is very natural. To
feel for thirty-seven years an innate antipathy for
the married state, and then suddenly through the
force of circumstances to be driven into it, without
being in the slightest degree captivated by one's
bride—is fearful. In order to get used to the

idea and pull myself together a little, I decided
not to abandon my original plan and to go into
the country for a month. I did so. The quiet
country life amid those very dear to me had a
beneficial effect. I quieted myself with the
reflection that no one can escape his destiny and
that there was something fatalistic in my meeting
with this girl. . . . God knows, I have the purest
intentions with regard to my life-companion. If
we are both unhappy, it won't be my fault. My
conscience is clear. If I marry without love . . .
it is because I could do nothing else'.

To Kashkin, years afterwards, Tchaïkovsky
gave another, fantastically ingenious account—so
typical that it must be summarized. He had
ignored and forgotten Antonina's first letter (in April,
before *Onegin* was thought about), he told
Kashkin, but when the second came, threatening
suicide if that too were ignored, he was almost
superstitiously impressed by the parallel between
real life and the situation which had chiefly
attracted him to Pushkin's poem: the letter
scene. 'I was in love with Tatyana and furious
with Onegin for his coldness and heartlessness'.
And here was a Tatyana in real life. Could he
behave like Onegin, worse than Onegin? Then
having agreed to this Platonic marriage, vaguely
hoping that somehow everything would turn out
for the best, he went to Glebovo, plunged happily
into *Onegin*—and almost put the thought of
Antonina from his mind! 'Only somewhere deep
within me stirred an uneasy expectation of some-

thing I didn't want to think about'. At any rate,
a letter from Antonina sharply brought him back
to unpleasant reality.

He went to Moscow, lying to Shilovsky that he
was obliged to visit his eighty - three - year - old
father in Petersburg, and on July 6th/18th was
married. His father sent his blessing, but Anatol
was the only member of the family who went to
Moscow for the ceremony, while none of his
Conservatoire colleagues knew anything about it
till after. The unhappy bridegroom at once
found that he had bound himself for life to a
woman who would always be a stranger to him,
not only physically but intellectually: 'She did
not once show the slightest wish to know what I
was doing, what my work was, my plans, what
I was reading, what I was fond of in intellectual
and artistic matters. Among other things, the
following circumstance particularly astonished
me. She told me she had been in love with me
for four years; and that she was a very respectable
musician. Just imagine that, for all that, she
knew *not a single note of my compositions* and only on
the very eve of my flight asked me which of my
piano pieces she could buy at Jurgenson's. This
fact absolutely nonplussed me. I was no less
surprised to learn from her that she had never
been to the concerts and quartet performances of
the Mus. Soc., though she must surely have known
that she could always see there the object of her
four years' love and though there was nothing to
prevent her going. You naturally ask how we

spent the time when we were left alone together?
She talked a great deal, but her conversation
always led to the following few subjects. She
constantly repeated to me innumerable tales of
the innumerable men in whom she had aroused
tender emotions. For the most part they were
generals, nephews of famous bankers, well-known
artists, even members of the Imperial family. . . .'
Still, he claimed: 'I sincerely wished and tried to
be a good husband'.

After a week in Petersburg, they paid a visit to
Antonina's mother, then separated for about a
month, he going to his sister at Kamenka (lying to
his wife that he was obliged to take a cure in the
Caucasus), she to Moscow to prepare their home.
'A few days longer and I swear I should have
gone mad'. But Kamenka soon exercised a
calming effect; he 'again breathed freely'; after
a couple of weeks he felt 'decidedly better . . .
convinced that I shall now triumph over my rather
difficult and critical situation. I must fight down
the feeling of *estrangement* from my wife and think
of her good qualities'. 'I feel so much better
that I have begun the instrumentation of *your*
Symphony', he wrote to Mme. von Meck. And he
also completed the draft of *Eugene Onegin* and
began to orchestrate that, too. By the time he
rejoined his wife in Moscow he had finished the
scoring of the first movement of the Symphony.

His first impression of his new home was
favourable. It was 'nice and comfortable', he
thought. He appeared at the Conservatoire,

obviously battling hard with his nerves, but avoided conversation with his colleagues, rushing home the moment his classes were over. On one occasion only did the newly married pair appear together socially one evening at Jurgenson's, when Antonina was introduced to her husband's friends. She struck them all as pleasant but 'unreal', 'a sort of conserve', as Nicholas Rubinstein said—while her husband hardly left her side, nervously interfering when she tried to converse and completing her unfinished sentences for her. But this strained position lasted barely a fortnight. Tchaïkovsky made up his mind that suicide was the only way out, and sought some method of suicide which might be disguised as a natural death. One bitterly cold night, he told Kashkin later, he waded into the river 'almost up to the waist', hoping to catch pneumonia, and told Antonina, on his return, that he had been fishing and fallen in accidentally. But his robust physique defeated him.

Finally, having induced Anatol to send a faked telegram in Napravnik's name, he fled to Petersburg on September 24th/October 6th 'in a state bordering on insanity'. Anatol met his brother at the station and hardly recognized him, 'his face had so changed in the course of a month'. Anatol took him straight to an hotel, where, after a terrible nerve-storm, he lay unconscious for nearly forty-eight hours. The verdict of the doctor, a mental specialist, was that nothing but complete change would save his reason; there must be no attempt at renewal of conjugal relations and it would be advisable for Tchaïkovsky never even to see his wife again. Anatol at once hurried to Moscow to break the news to Antonina, and Nicholas Rubinstein, who accompanied him, told her everything with brutal frankness. But she received the news with perfect calm, even indifference; said she would 'bear anything for Peti's sake'; poured out tea; and when left alone with Anatol merely remarked pleasantly, 'Well, I never expected that Rubinstein would drink tea with me to-day'. In later years she used to write her husband long, half-meaningless, blackmailing letters, and in 1917 she died in a lunatic asylum where she had been confined for more than twenty years. It is not impossible that the seeds of insanity were already present in her mind in 1877. Fate can have played few more fantastic pranks than this marriage of a homosexual to a nymphomaniac.

Was Tchaïkovsky's abnormality congenital or the result of environment—perhaps at the School of Jurisprudence? Probably the former. As a boy, like other natural homosexuals, he showed an abnormal and unhealthy affection for his mother, who died when he was fourteen; and here, perhaps, we have the clue to his side of the extraordinary spiritual 'love-affair' which gradually developed with Nadezhda von Meck, who apparently answered in his imagination to that 'certain need for tenderness and care which only a woman can satisfy' which he felt and which sometimes filled him with 'mad longing'. And, despite the unusual amount of affection he often showed toward males, there is little ground for supposing that he was a 'practising' homosexual. He appears to have exercised great self-control and was obviously profoundly ashamed of his abnormality.

CHAPTER V

1877–84

At Clarens – annuity from Mme. von Meck – Fourth Symphony and *Onegin* completed at San Remo – Tchaïkovsky's criticisms of the Balakirev group – Piano Sonata and Violin Concerto written at Clarens and Kamenka – 'dreamlike life' at Brailov –Liturgy of St. John Chrysostom – First Orchestral Suite – temporarily resumes work at the Conservatoire – resignation – work on *Maid of Orleans* in Florence and at Clarens – hears *The Tempest* in Paris – *Onegin* performed by Moscow students – reappearance of Antonina – Second Piano Concerto – father's death – Second Symphony rewritten and *Italian Capriccio* composed in Rome – learns English – falling off in productivity – *The Year 1812* and Serenade for Strings – death of Nicholas Rubinstein – Tchaïkovsky declines the Directorship of the Moscow Conservatoire – edits Bortnyansky's works – Brodsky plays the Violin Concerto – Trio in memory of Rubinstein – annoyance at Rimsky-Korsakov's *Snow Maiden* – begins *Mazeppa* – the Moscow Exhibition – depression – renewal of correspondence with Balakirev – music for the coronation of Alexander III – Second Orchestral Suite – Tchaïkovsky absent from Petersburg *première* of *Mazeppa* – relations with the Tsar.

AFTER the marriage *débâcle*, Tchaïkovsky and his brother Anatol made first for Clarens, on the shores of Lake Geneva. They had money for only a few weeks' stay, but Peter was far too upset to be able to return to Moscow and he was literally at his wits' end. It was at this juncture that Nadezhda von Meck, who had already paid his debts to the tune of three thousand rubles, induced him to accept an annuity of six thousand rubles (rather more than £600), thus freeing him from all financial anxiety and enabling him, on his recovery, to devote the whole of his time to creative work. Deeply touched, Tchaïkovsky

wrote that in future every note from his pen
should be dedicated to her. It was the beginning of an entirely new phase of his life. Early
in November the brothers left for Italy—Milan,
Florence, Rome, Venice—Peter still ill, terribly
depressed and with fearfully exacerbated nerves,
unable to bear the least noise, furious even with
the newsvendors who cried news of Turkish
successes in the Russo-Turkish War. One night
he drank two bottles of neat brandy in a vain
attempt to induce oblivion, and lay sleepless till
morning, fully conscious but 'in a condition more
awful than anything I ever experienced before or
since', he told Kashkin.

Yet even before leaving Clarens he had finished
the orchestration of the first act of *Onegin*, and in
Venice he began the scoring of the second. Early
in December Anatol had to return to Russia, and
Peter accompanied him as far as Vienna, where
he was bored by *Die Walküre* and Brahms's 'cold,
obscure, pretentious' First Symphony, but quite
enchanted by Delibes' *Sylvia*. He always preferred French composers, above all Bizet and
Delibes, to their greater German contemporaries.
(Presumably the explanation lies in his own
French blood, which from this period onward
left ever deeper marks on his own music.) With
his young servant Sofronov, sent from Russia to
take Anatol's place, he returned to Venice and
then moved on to San Remo, finishing there the
score of the Fourth Symphony, 'the best thing I've
written up to now', on December 26th, 1877/

January 7th, 1878. The score was sent to Russia and performed with very mild success at an R.M.S. Concert in Moscow six weeks later.* The Symphony off his mind, he resumed the scoring of *Onegin* and finished that work, too, on January 20th/February 1st. In San Remo he was joined by the other twin, Modest, with the latter's pupil.

And it was from San Remo that he sent Mme. von Meck that long letter, scathingly attacking Balakirev and the rest of the 'handful', except Rimsky-Korsakov, which has too often been quoted as an expression of his final judgement on the Petersburg group. It may have been a sincere statement of his view at that time, unbalanced as he was. But apart from its inaccuracies on points of fact, it contrasts curiously with many statements in other letters. He speaks of Rimsky-Korsakov's Quartet, Op. 12, for instance, as 'permeated with a character of dry pedantry' —which is certainly true. Yet fifteen months before he had told Rimsky-Korsakov himself that the first movement is 'simply delightful . . . a model of purity of style', the slow movement 'rather dry, but on that account very characteristic—as a reminiscence of the *Zopf* period', the scherzo 'very lively and piquant; it must sound very beautiful', and criticizing only the finale. If this letter to Rimsky-Korsakov is not to be dismissed as mere insincere flattery, either Tchaïkovsky must have changed his mind (as he rarely did) about a work which, in his own words, 'improved with closer acquaintance', or the later

letter to Mme. von Meck must be accepted only
as the reflection of a mood of 'mental and physical
illness'. There is a peculiar irony, moreover, in
his references to Balakirev as a man of enormous
talent whose career was already over with little
accomplished. For Tchaïkovsky, as we shall see,
was once more to fall to some extent under
Balakirev's influence for a time. And some of
Balakirev's most important works were written
long after Tchaïkovsky himself was in the
grave.

In February the party moved to Florence, in
March back to Clarens, where Tchaïkovsky began
two large-scale works, his Piano Sonata and the
Violin Concerto, completing both, orchestration
and all, by the end of April at home at Kamenka.
In May, Mme. von Meck offered him the tem-
porary use of her great house at Brailov. In her
absence the entire establishment was placed at his
disposal. It was 'a wonderful dreamlike life',
and in these luxurious surroundings he completed
his most important piece of religious music, the
setting of the Liturgy of St. John Chrysostom,
which as literature he considered 'one of the
greatest works of art in existence'. Tchaïkovsky's
attitude to the Orthodox Church resembled
Rimsky-Korsakov's in one respect : he could not
accept its dogmas but, as an artistic experience,
he found in its services 'one of my greatest joys'.
At Brailov, too, he brooded over other opera
subjects—*Romeo and Juliet* or even another *Undine*
—and wept over *Onegin* as he played it to himself.

The summer passed in a round of visits to Nizy, Kamenka and Verbovka (where in August he sketched out an orchestral Suite, Op. 43, 'in Lachner's manner').

In September he returned to Moscow just a year after the catastrophe and resumed his Conservatoire work, though determined to resign as soon as he decently could and, opening the door unlocked by Mme. von Meck, to make the fullest use of his freedom. But it was impossible to do anything for the moment, for Nicholas Rubinstein was still in Paris conducting concerts of Russian music (including Tchaïkovsky's *Tempest* and the Piano Concerto) at the International Exhibition, a commission which Tchaïkovsky himself had been offered and refused the previous winter. When Tchaïkovsky did announce his intention to Rubinstein he was amusingly disappointed at the latter's failure to explode with indignation, or even to try to persuade him to change his mind. 'It turned out quite otherwise. He listened to me laughingly as one listens to a headstrong child, and expressed no regret'. (Rubinstein had already frankly revealed his disbelief in the seriousness of Tchaïkovsky's breakdown and accused him during the past winter of running away from life and its difficulties.) 'He only remarked that the Conservatoire would lose *a lot of its prestige* with the withdrawal of my name— a polite way of saying that the pupils wouldn't lose much through my resignation. He is quite right, for I'm really a bad, unintelligent teacher

—and yet I had expected more opposition from
him'.

After a few weeks in Petersburg and at
Kamenka, the now free composer went to Italy
at the end of November, 1878. Mme. von Meck
had taken a suite of rooms for him in Florence,
where she was staying herself and where he
frequently saw her—at a distance—and there he
finished his orchestral Suite. But he was eager
to press on with a new opera, based on Zhukov-
sky's translation of Schiller's *Jungfrau von Orleans*,
and, needing more quiet than he could find in
Florence, returned at the beginning of 1879 to
the Villa Richelieu at Clarens. On this occasion
he prepared his own libretto, work which gave
him infinitely more trouble than the writing of
the music, but the whole opera—one of his
feeblest works, though certainly free from the
'Russianism' he feared might have crept into it
—was completed on February 21st/March 5th.
By that time he was in Paris. To flee to Clarens
for peace and then to Paris for 'brilliance, noise
and distraction'—that was typical of Tchaïkovsky.
But even in Paris he avoided calling on acquaintances: Turgenev, Saint-Saëns and others. 'Every
new acquaintanceship', he wrote, 'every fresh
meeting with someone unknown has always been
for me a source of fearful moral suffering . . .
springing possibly from a shyness which has
increased to a mania, perhaps from complete lack
of any need for human society, perhaps also from
inability, without an effort, to say things about

oneself that one doesn't think (which is unavoidable in social intercourse)—in short, I don't know what it is. As long as I was not in a position to avoid such meetings, I went into society, pretended to enjoy myself, constantly played a part (as one must)—and suffered the most fearful torments. . . . The society of a fellow-creature is pleasant only when long-standing intimacy or community of interests makes it possible to dispense with all effort'. But Tchaïkovsky liked the atmosphere of Paris; he was happy in reading Rousseau's *Confessions* and finding his own image (he says) reflected in so many of their pages; but then he heard his *Tempest* feebly applauded and feebly hissed at a Châtelet Concert—and hurried back to Russia. Though not before the ever-sincere one, the despiser of Liszt's 'Jesuitry', had sent Colonne a curious letter regretting that his 'state of health had prevented his expressing his gratitude personally', and beginning with the rather strange statement that 'by chance, I came to Paris on the very day you were kind enough to perform my *Tempest*'. Tchaïkovsky never shirked a convenient lie—and often naïvely confessed to one. He told Jurgenson, for instance, how he once got rid of an unwelcome acquaintance encountered on a train-journey, by saying that he was travelling with a lady. But the lie to Colonne seems so unnecessary.

On March 17th/29th Tchaïkovsky heard the first performance of *Eugene Onegin*, given by the students of the Moscow Conservatoire. Even

Anton Rubinstein came specially from Petersburg to hear the work, though as usual he was little impressed. The success as a whole was purely one of 'esteem'. And a visit to Petersburg a few days later involved the composer in an unpleasant encounter, or rather series of encounters, with his wife, who tried to reassert her conjugal rights and had to be bought off.

The summer of 1879, devoted to the addition of a sixth movement to the orchestral Suite and to the scoring of *The Maid of Orleans*, was again divided between Kamenka, Brailov and Simaki. This last-named estate was a smaller property of Mme. von Meck's, not far from Brailov, where Nadezhda herself came in August. This proximity to his benefactress disturbed Tchaïkovsky terribly, and one day 'something very painful' happened; they met by accident in the woods. 'It was very upsetting. Although we were face to face only for a brief moment, I was none the less confused. I raised my hat, while she seemed to lose her head entirely and didn't know what to do'.

At the end of November Tchaïkovsky again escaped with joy and relief from the native land of which he thought with such passionate love whenever he was far from it. After a week or so in Paris (where he finished the sketch of his Second Piano Concerto in G, a work of which none of our concert pianists has apparently ever heard) and a few days in Turin he reached Rome in the second week of December. There he

received the news of his father's death. He wept.
But he seems to have been far more upset by the
fact that no one in Moscow had wired him 'a
few words of appreciation' after the first performance of his Suite. 'The sole interest which binds
me to life is—my activity as a composer. Every
first performance of my works marks an epoch
for me. . . . My nerves are upset and I'm as sick
as a dog'. In Rome he drastically revised the
Second Symphony, writing an almost entirely
new first movement, which according to Taneev
is far inferior to the original one, and composed
the *Italian Capriccio*, based on folk-melodies and
opening with a trumpet-call heard each evening
from the cavalry barracks near his hotel. The
scoring was finished in the summer at Kamenka.

Shortly after his return to Petersburg in March,
1880, Tchaïkovsky made the acquaintance of the
twenty-two-year-old Grand Duke Constantine
Constantinovich, son of the music-loving Grand
Duke Constantine Nikolaevich, and himself a
passionate admirer of Tchaïkovsky's music. The
young prince afterwards corresponded with the
composer and some of Tchaïkovsky's later songs
are settings of the Grand Duke's verses. The
summer passed uneventfully, divided as usual
between Kamenka, Brailov and Simaki. At
Simaki Tchaïkovsky began to learn English,
studying to such purpose that he afterwards
managed to read *David Copperfield*, *Bleak House* and
his favourite *Pickwick* in the original. (Among
the occasional English phrases sprinkled through

his diary, one notes the Wellerian 'wery'.) He was at this period suffering, as Rimsky-Korsakov did a few years later, from a fever for revising his earlier works and for projecting monographs on composers, histories of music, and so on. Hitherto he had always sneered at those composers who worked only when they were in the mood, instead of regularly like craftsmen, 'like cobblers'; but he now recognized the danger of continually trying to 'meet inspiration half-way' and of becoming a mere composing-machine. Accordingly, we find a considerable falling off in the quantity of his production during the next year or two. Nevertheless, at Kamenka in October he wrote two biggish works in a great hurry, the *1812* Overture commissioned for the forthcoming Moscow Exhibition ('very noisy . . . written without much enthusiasm . . . and probably of no great artistic value') and the Serenade for Strings, Op. 48 ('written from an inward impulse' and always rather a favourite work of the composer's). The two compositions have nothing in common but the employment of folk-songs. Three of Tchaïkovsky's works were heard for the first time in December and January—the Serenade, the *Italian Capriccio* and the Liturgy of St. John Chrysostom—and on January 11th/23rd, 1881, *Eugene Onegin* was given in Moscow, this time by professionals, though still without marked success.

On February 13th/25th, *The Maid of Orleans*, too, was produced at the Maryinsky Theatre, Petersburg, after prolonged battles with the

Direction, the singers and that knight of the baton
and blue pencil, Eduard Napravnik, to whom the
work was dedicated. Tchaïkovsky was recalled
no fewer than twenty-four times, but the critics
unanimously damned the thing and it was with-
drawn from the repertory. The day after the
production Tchaïkovsky left for Italy. Within
two or three weeks he was lunching with the
young Grand Duke Constantine and his cousins
in Rome, and the three princes proposed to take
him with them to Athens and Jerusalem. But
the news of the assassination of Alexander II put
an end to this plan by sending them back to
Russia. Hardly more than a week later Tchaïkovsky learned of another death which affected
him more closely. Nicholas Rubinstein, who was
to have joined him at Nice, died in Paris on
March 11th/23rd (just five days before Mussorgsky), and Tchaïkovsky hastened there, 'suffering less, I must confess to my shame, from the
sense of fearful, irreparable loss than from the
fear of seeing poor Rubinstein's body'. He was
also worried by the news that Mme. von Meck
had suffered very heavy financial losses, caused
by the extravagance of her son, Vladimir, and
that his allowance might therefore be endangered.
But for the time being she insisted on continuing
it, and in spite of this possible embarrassment
Tchaïkovsky declined 'most emphatically' the
Directorship of the Moscow Conservatoire, offered
him in succession to Rubinstein.

He spent almost the whole of the summer,

from May to October, at Kamenka. Alexandra
('Sasha') was ill and away with her husband, so
that Peter was obliged to act as 'head of the
family' and look after the children, of whom he
was very fond. During the whole of this period
he felt no desire to compose and even began to
wonder whether he had not written himself out.
He whiled away the time by studying the music,
rites and ceremonials of the Orthodox Church
and by editing for Jurgenson the works of
Bortnyansky, which he detested. But apparently he was glad to earn a little money by this
means. Indeed, he was so worried about his
financial position—with how much justification,
it is difficult to say—that he secretly wrote to the
young Tsar asking for help, and received a present
of three hundred rubles. In November he left
again for Rome, where he almost immediately
received news of the first performance of his Violin
Concerto, totally ignored for two years. Neither
Auer, to whom it was originally dedicated, nor
Tchaïkovsky's more intimate friend Kotek, would
have anything to do with it. But now Brodsky
had chosen it for his début in Vienna, where it
aroused a storm of criticism. Hanslick's notice
was particularly devastating; according to his
brother, Tchaïkovsky 'was never able to forget it
to the end of his life and even knew it by heart,
just as he remembered a criticism of Cui's dating
from 1866'. (This must have been Cui's attack
on his leaving cantata, *An die Freude*.)

In Rome, Tchaïkovsky began to compose again

embarking on a work for a combination—piano, violin and 'cello—which he had more than once declared was 'torture' to have to listen to. He was now drawn to it, not because he had overcome his antipathy, but principally because he wished to dedicate to the memory of Nicholas Rubinstein a work of more or less intimate nature with an important piano part. But he informed Nadezhda von Meck that he had reconciled himself to the combination solely in the hope of pleasing her, whom he knew to be a lover of piano trios.[1] The lengthy variations which form the second part of the Trio are, in a sense, 'enigma' variations, for not only had the theme a private association with Rubinstein but each variation refers to some episode in Rubinstein's career, though the details have never been revealed. The Trio, dedicated 'To the Memory of a Great Artist', was completed by the middle of January, 1882.

Tchaïkovsky's health was, for the time being, much better and he had nothing to worry about but affairs in Russia—the Nihilists ('who ought to be exterminated'), his sister's illness and the poor success of his operas. 'But what angers me fearfully, and hurts and mortifies me', he wrote to Jurgenson, 'is the fact that the Theatre Directorate which wouldn't spend a kopek on

[1] It is true she had suggested in October, 1880, that he should write something for her private trio, of which the pianist at that time was none other than Claude Debussy. (Debussy visited Moscow in the summer of 1881, but Tchaïkovsky was at Kamenka and they never met.)

The Maid of Orleans has granted thirty thousand
rubles for the production of Rimsky-Korsakov's
Snow Maiden. Isn't it also unpleasant to you that
this subject has been torn from us and that Lel
will now sing new music to the old words; that
they have, as it were, taken by force a piece of
myself and are going to offer it to the public in
a new dress? I could cry with mortification'.
He spent the greater part of February and March,
1882, at Naples with Modest, happy but inactive,
tormented not by nerves but by organ-grinders,
mice — of which he was terrified — and the
ubiquitous Neapolitan beggars.

At Kamenka, where he again spent practically
the whole of the summer, he began in May to
work—though with little enthusiasm—at a new
opera, *Mazeppa*, based on Pushkin's poem, *Poltava*.
About a year before K. Y. Davidov—the 'cello
virtuoso and head of the Petersburg Conservatoire,
not one of his brother-in-law's family—had given
him Burenin's libretto on this subject, but it had
not appealed to him. Even now he took it up
only for want of something better and made very
heavy going of the composition. 'Never has any
important work given me such trouble as this
opera', he writes in September. And again at
the end of October, when the actual composition
was finished and he was merely orchestrating:
'*Mazeppa* progresses at a snail's pace, though I
work at it several hours a day'. And he was
unable to decide whether this was due to loss of
powers or to increasing severity of self-criticism.

The Art and Industrial Exhibition in Moscow that summer also brought several first performances of his works: the Second Piano Concerto, with Taneev as soloist, the *1812* Overture, specially written for the Exhibition, and the Violin Concerto, again with Brodsky, now heard for the first time in Russia. One Exhibition concert was entirely devoted to his works. This drew him to Moscow for a few days and as usual the city ('for which I feel such keen affection, although I can't live in it') brought on a terrible fit of depression dispelled only by return to Kamenka. 'The fact is', he wrote to Modest, 'that life is impossible for me, except in the country or abroad. Why this is—God knows, I don't understand—but I'm on the verge of insanity. This indefinable, horrible, torturing malady of not being able to spend a single day, a single hour, in either of the Russian capitals without suffering, will one of these days be the cause of my promotion to a better world. . . . I often think that the whole of my discontent is due to the fact that I am very egotistic, that I am unable to sacrifice myself for others, even those near and dear to me. Then it occurs to me that I certainly shouldn't have willingly submitted to moral torments if I didn't regard it as a sort of duty to come here now and again so as to give pleasure to others'.

That autumn Tchaïkovsky renewed his correspondence with Balakirev after the ten years' break. About a year before, Tchaïkovsky had written him with regard to the new edition of

Romeo and Juliet but without receiving a reply.
Now Balakirev wrote, without the slightest refer-
ence to his little delay, expressing pleasure that
the other had not forgotten him and characteristically announcing:. 'I've got a programme for
a symphony, which you'd carry out splendidly'.
To which Tchaïkovsky replied in terms difficult
to reconcile with the San Remo letter of 1877:
'It would have been strange if I had "*erased you
from my affectionate memory!*" Apart altogether
from the sincere respect for you, both as man and
musician, which I should have felt even if fate
had never brought us into contact—would it be
possible for me not to value the innumerable
tokens of friendly sympathy you have shown me?
I can tell you without any exaggeration that if
another ten or twenty years passed without my
seeing you, it would be just the same. I should
never forget you or cease to think of you with
affection as one of the most brilliant, absolutely
true and gifted artistic personalities I have ever
met. I thank you cordially for your intention to
suggest a subject for a symphonic poem. . . .
When I am in Petersburg, of course I will come
and see you'. But since that might not be for
some months, 'won't you outline the proposed
subject by letter? I'm very interested. I can
promise definitely that, if my mental and physical
health allow, I shall carry out the task you set
me with the greatest readiness'. (Although he
had written no programme-music since *Francesca*
five or six years before.) That was enough for

Balakirev. He at once replied, not only disclosing the proposed subject, Byron's *Manfred*, which he had suggested to Berlioz sixteen years earlier, and detailing the four-movement programme with a Berliozian *idée fixe*, which in the end Tchaïkovsky followed almost exactly, but characteristically laying down a key-scheme for him as well. But Tchaïkovsky did not at first care for the subject and said so frankly. There, for the time being, the matter rested. But he took the opportunity to tell Balakirev he could not agree that *The Tempest* and *Francesca* were, as Balakirev considered, the 'apogee' of his work. On the contrary, in his own view they were 'really extremely cold, false and weak'.

In January, 1883, Tchaïkovsky joined Modest in Paris, intending to spend the rest of the winter in Italy. (On the way he heard *Tristan* in Berlin —it was just a month before Wagner's death—and 'had never been so bored in his life'.) But while in Paris he received two commissions which had to be executed at once. The coronation of Alexander III was to take place in Moscow in May and Tchaïkovsky had already been instructed to arrange the 'Slavsya' from *A Life for the Tsar* to be sung by a chorus of thousands of students as a greeting to the Tsar and Tsaritsa, as they entered the Kremlin. Now he received the libretto of a coronation cantata, *Moscow*, from the Coronation Committee, with a request that he would set it by the middle of April, and another commission from the city of Moscow for a march to be performed at a fête in the Sokolniky Park the week after the coronation. As an intensely loyal subject, and in gratitude for the Tsar's secret gift of three hundred rubles, he undertook both works but refused to accept any fee for them. All the work was done in Paris and Tchaïkovsky returned to Russia only on the eve of the coronation. During the summer and autumn, he wrote his Second Orchestral Suite, Op. 53, not because he was 'inspired' but because he was tired of waiting for inspiration; it was confessedly a product of mere *cacoëthes scribendi*. That finished, he 'feverishly' resumed his English study in his 'impatience to be able to read Dickens fluently'.

Tchaïkovsky was now definitely established in the favour of the Imperial family; *Eugene Onegin* was Alexander III's favourite opera; and Vsevolozhsky, the new Director of the Theatres, being extremely well disposed towards him, *Mazeppa* was produced almost simultaneously in both capitals—in Moscow on February 3rd/15th, 1884, in Petersburg four days later—winning in both cases mere *succès d'estime*. Tchaïkovsky attended the Moscow performance but, too nervous to go to Petersburg, left the next day for Paris, not even waiting in Moscow to hear Erdmannsdörfer conduct his Second Suite for the first time that very evening. The young Tsar attended the Petersburg *première*, staying to the end, and expressed his 'extreme surprise' at the composer's absence. Jurgenson wrote to the fugitive, bluntly telling him that *Mazeppa* had failed and that he himself was largely to blame through his non-attendance. To which the composer humbly replied that he 'knew better than anyone how he paralysed his success owing to his unfortunate temperament'. Napravnik wrote him in much the same strain. Then came the news that the Tsar had conferred on him the Order of St. Vladimir (Fourth Class) and the unhappy runaway, who believed the failure of his opera to be far worse than it actually was, was hauled home from Paris to receive the decoration.

Well dosed with bromide, he was presented to the Tsar and Tsaritsa at Gachina on March 7th/19th. 'Both were most friendly and kind. I believe that anyone who has even a single opportunity to look into the Emperor's eyes will remain for ever his passionate admirer, for it is difficult to give any idea of the charm and sympathy of his whole manner'. Tchaïkovsky had always been a very mild liberal in politics, a detester of nihilists and a believer in the 'very gradual' abolition of autocracy and substitution of parliamentary government 'when everyone would feel happy'. But by 1885, 'although not yet one of the ultra-conservatives', he had 'become very doubtful of the perfect utility of these institutions', i.e. parliaments. He was 'firmly convinced that the welfare of the majority depends not on *principles* and *theories* but on those individuals who happen to be at the head of affairs. . . . Now have we such a *man* in whom we can trust? I

reply: Yes—the Sovereign. He has fascinated
me—as a personality; but apart from that, I
think the Tsar is a good man. I like his caution
in introducing the new and doing away with the
old'.

CHAPTER VI

1884–90

Concert Fantasia and Third Orchestral Suite – success of *Onegin* in Petersburg – religious discussions with Balakirev – at Davos – takes a house at Maidanovo – *Vakula the Smith* revised as *The Little Shoes* – *Manfred* and Tchaïkovsky's duplicity – *The Sorceress* – Tchaïkovsky's household – his daily routine – visit to Tiflis – begins to conduct again – *Mozartiana* – sets out on conducting tour – meetings with Desirée Artôt, Brahms, Grieg and Ethel Smyth – visits Hamburg, Prague, Paris and London – moves to Frolovskoe – Fifth Symphony – *Hamlet* Overture – *The Sleeping Beauty* – second European tour – writes *The Queen of Spades* in Florence – String Sextet.

In April, 1884, Tchaïkovsky began two new works, the Concert Fantasia for piano and orchestra, Op. 56, and the Third Orchestral Suite (with its famous variations), which he dedicated to Erdmannsdörfer in gratitude for that conductor's success with the Second Suite. The new Suite was originally conceived as a symphony and its original first movement became the second movement of the Concert Fantasia, both works being written in a rather laboured way. The composer spent September at Pleshcheevo, a smaller property which Nadezhda von Meck had bought after the sale of Brailov, necessitated by her losses, and there made the acquaintance of Mussorgsky's *Khovanshchina*, in which he found 'what I expected—very peculiarly conceived realism, wretched technique, poverty of invention and some clever episodes in an ocean of harmonic absurdities and mannerisms'. Which is rather strange, for the *Khovanshchina* that Tchaïkovsky knew, as tidied up by Rimsky-Korsakov, is a singularly respectable piece of work, as Tchaïkovsky would have seen if he had not been blinded by preconceived ideas.

On October 19th/31st, at the Tsar's command, *Eugene Onegin* was given for the first time on the Imperial stage in Petersburg. (It had already been given in Petersburg by amateurs.) It had a poor press. But the public liked it, the Tsar was known to have given it the *cachet* of his approval, and from the second performance twelve days later the work enjoyed enormous popularity. There is a pleasant irony in the fact that the one opera which Tchaïkovsky wrote almost without any thought of its production, indeed loving the characters so intensely that it was distasteful to him to think of their being vulgarized by a stage performance, brought him wide popularity and swelled his bank-account. He attended the first two performances and, according to Modest, became much more sociable again at this period. He no longer avoided people and shirked public duties, but revived old friendships and made many new ones. At any rate it was during this visit to Petersburg that he renewed personal contact with Balakirev and Stassov.

With Balakirev he plunged into discussions of religion and of church-music, the Emperor having hinted that he would like Tchaïkovsky to write for the Church. On the eve of his departure for

Switzerland, Tchaïkovsky sent Balakirev a note in which he speaks of being 'deeply touched by our conversation of yesterday'. 'How good you are!' he goes on. 'What a true friend you are to me! How I wish that that transfiguration which has been effected in your soul might be vouchsafed also to mine. I can say without the slightest infringement of the truth that I *thirst* more than ever for peace and support in *Christ*. Pray that I may be strengthened in my faith in Him'. One wonders if he complied with Balakirev's request: 'If you have a free half-hour to-day, don't refuse to hurry for a few moments to Glinka's sister, Lyudmila Ivanovna Shestakova, who lives near you. . . . She is ill and confined to her house and your visit (even if a very short one) would give her *enormous pleasure*, and besides it's always nice to give pleasure to others. She has chosen your *Romeo and Juliet* Overture for performance at the unveiling of the Glinka monument at Smolensk. Please don't refuse my request, for Lyudmila Ivanovna is old and ill and it's hardly likely that you'll have another chance to see her'. Actually, Lyudmila Shestakova outlived Tchaïkovsky by thirteen years.

The question of *Manfred* came up again before Tchaïkovsky left; Balakirev sent him a fresh key-scheme, disregarded like the former one, advice to include the organ at the end (which he did) and—a list of the compositions he was to take as his models in each movement. Tchaïkovsky was now more attracted by the subject. He bought a copy of the poem and set off for Davos with it in his luggage, the morning after the second performance of *Onegin*. His object in visiting Switzerland was not, however, to get local colour for *Manfred*—although, as he said, his stay among the Alps 'ought to have a very beneficial effect on the musical incarnation of Manfred'—but to visit Kotek, who lay dying of consumption at Davos. (He lived only a month or so longer.) At Davos Tchaïkovsky read *Manfred* and wrote to Balakirev promising that the symphony should be written 'not later than the summer'. He also sent some of the church-music composed at the Tsar's wish, for Balakirev's use in the Imperial Chapel—and as in the old days received some very frank criticism.

From Davos Tchaïkovsky drifted on to Paris, more than ever dissatisfied with his homeless condition. The summer before he had told Nadezhda von Meck that he wanted to take a small house of his own in the country. It must stand alone, have a nice garden—if possible with a stream, be near a forest, and not too far from a railway station so that he could get to Moscow without difficulty. He now wrote to Modest from Paris of his 'homesickness, the desire for a place of my own. Life abroad has become loathsome. . . . I must have a *home*, be it at Kamenka or in Moscow—at any rate I can't go on living like a wandering star'. Soon after his return to Russia, his servant found him a rather large furnished house which answered most of his requirements, at Maidanovo, not far from Klin, a town within easy reach of Moscow.

He settled at Maidanovo in February, 1885, under the happiest auspices. True, he was suffering from severe headaches, but he was no longer the neurotic weakling of the last few years. The Third Suite had just scored a tremendous triumph under Hans von Bülow in Petersburg, and one nearly as great under Erdmannsdörfer in Moscow a few days later. The Tsar had sent for him after another performance of *Onegin*, conversed with him for a long time in the most friendly way, inquiring about his life and work; the Tsaritsa, too, had been most kind. He had just been elected head of the Moscow branch of the R.M.S., while his enormous correspondence convinced him of his widespread popularity. And he was satisfied with the drastic revision of *Vakula the Smith*, at which he had been working since November, clarifying, cutting and adding new numbers. In its new form the work was rechristened *Cherevichki* (i.e. *The Little Shoes*), though it is also known outside Russia as *Oxana's Caprices*. He had just induced the dramatist Shpazhinsky to prepare a libretto from his play, *The Sorceress*. But Shpazhinsky delayed with his first act, and in April Tchaïkovsky started instead to redeem his promise to Balakirev by beginning *Manfred*. (The work was dedicated to Balakirev and Tchaïkovsky seems to have gone out of his way, particularly in the scherzo, to write in a pseudo-Balakirevian vein.)

Tchaïkovsky once confided to his diary his
conviction that 'letters are not usually altogether
sincere. At least, I judge by myself. To whom-
ever I write, and whatever I write about, I always
worry about the impression the letter will make,
not only on my correspondent but on any chance
reader. Consequently I pose. Sometimes I *strive*
to make the tone of the letter simple and sincere,
i.e. to make it *appear* so. But, except letters written
in moments of *aberration*, I am never my true self
in my correspondence. These letters are constant
sources of remorse and regret, sometimes even
very painful ones. When I read the letters of
celebrated people, printed posthumously, I am
always jarred by an indefinable feeling of falsity
and mendacity'. The reader of Tchaïkovsky's
own correspondence certainly receives a good
many jars of that nature. The composer's habit
of saying one thing to one person and another to
someone else is very well illustrated by two letters
written on the same day in June, 1885, to Taneev,
who was no friend of Balakirev's, and to Mme.
von Meck. He tells Nadezhda that he 'has
already taken such a fancy to this composition
that the opera will probably have to wait for
some time', and that although he feels it would
be a good thing 'to write nothing, travel, rest',
he is quite unable to tear himself from his writing-
table and piano. But he grumbles to Taneev
about his 'indiscreet promise' to Balakirev. 'It's
a thousand times pleasanter to write without
a programme. In writing a programme sym-

phony I feel as if I were a charlatan, cheating the public by giving it worthless paper instead of good coin'. Three or four months later Taneev rather maliciously told Balakirev about this, and Tchaïkovsky was at some pains to make peace: 'S. I. Taneev's tittle-tattle is mere childishness. . . . This is the real truth: generally speaking I don't like *my own* programme-music, as I've already told you. I feel infinitely freer in the sphere of pure symphony, and it's a hundred times easier for me to write something in the way of a *suite* than a programme thing. Frankly, I began *Manfred* with reluctance and decided to write it *simply* because I'd *promised* you. . . . The letter I wrote to Taneev refers to the time when I *began*—unwillingly, with an effort, with no self-confidence. . . . Then very quickly I was awfully attracted by *Manfred* and I don't remember ever experiencing such pleasure in work; and so it went on till the end'. Which, again, does not altogether agree with a remark to Mme. von Meck that 'the work is so difficult and complicated that at times I myself become a Manfred. . . . I'm straining all my powers to finish it as soon as possible: result—extreme exhaustion. That's the eternal "*cercle vicieux*" that I revolve in without finding a way out. If I have no work—I worry and get bored; when I have it, I work beyond my strength'. Surprisingly enough, he regarded *Manfred* for some time as the best of all his symphonic works, though he afterwards detested it, except the first movement.

Manfred was no sooner completed, early in September, than the composer began *The Sorceress*, finishing the first act in three weeks. At about the same time he moved to another, smaller house on the Maidanovo estate. It was unfurnished and most of the furnishing and arrangement was left to the servant, Sofronov, who surrounded his master with an extraordinary collection of rubbish. 'He himself', says Modest, 'assisted by buying utterly useless things—for instance, two horses which he had the greatest difficulty in selling again, and an old English clock that wouldn't go'. Sofronov's appalling taste did not worry him at all. 'He was as pleased as a child and boasted of his "own cook", "own washerwoman", "own silver", "own tablecloths" and "own dog" —all of which he considered extremely fine and praised to the skies'. He always expressed his delight in the very plain food prepared by his 'own cook', delight not always shared by his guests. Casual visitors were most unwelcome, but he liked to entertain his brothers or intimate friends—Laroche, Kashkin, Jurgenson, Taneev— though only when he was not engaged in composition. Not only did he need absolute solitude while creating, but from this time onward he became extremely secretive about his new works, never playing them or showing them even to his most intimate friends. Jurgenson's engraver was the first man to see his later scores.

At Maidanovo, too, he was able to adopt a routine from which he hardly ever deviated by

more than a minute or so, and never abandoned
when at home till the end of his life. He rose
between seven and eight, drank tea and read the
Bible, then studied English or read serious books
and took a short walk. He worked from half-past
nine to one o'clock, which was his dinner-hour.
After dinner, no matter what the weather, he took
a solitary two-hour walk, unaccompanied even by
a dog, and it was during these afternoon walks
that he did most of his creative work, jotting
down memoranda in innumerable little notebooks.
These notes were afterwards worked out at the
piano into the 'sketch' or reduced score, and his
full orchestra scores seldom differed materially
from the 'sketch'. When he was not composing
on his walks, he would recite aloud usually in
French. At four o'clock he had tea, worked from
five to seven; then took another walk, this time
with company if any were available, before supper
at eight o'clock. After supper he would read or
play cards—patience, if alone—talk or play the
piano till eleven, when he retired.

In April, 1886, a week or so after the first
performance of *Manfred* (in Moscow under
Erdmannsdörfer), Tchaïkovsky spent a month or
so at Tiflis, where Anatol was living, and where
Ippolitov-Ivanov had produced *Mazeppa* a few
months before. The scenery of the Caucasus
delighted him and the weeks he spent at Tiflis
were among the happiest of his life. The Tiflis
musicians organized an orchestral concert entirely
devoted to his works; the entire audience rose

and cheered as he entered the box at the theatre;
he was presented with wreaths and with an
address from the local Musical Society; and the
concert was followed by a supper in his honour.
So far it was the greatest triumph of his life
and, though only in a distant provincial city, he
appreciated it to the full. Having business in
Paris, he then made the sea-trip from Batum to
Marseilles, which he thoroughly enjoyed, made
himself much more agreeable to his French
colleagues than on previous visits to Paris, and
returned to Maidanovo in June, much refreshed
in mind and body. Within a couple of months
the sketches for *The Sorceress* were finished and the
orchestration begun. At about the same time,
Vsevolozhsky commissioned from him a ballet on
his old favourite, *Undine*, though for some reason
it was never written.

In December, 1886, after a terrible struggle
with his nerves, he conducted not only the
orchestral rehearsals of *The Little Shoes* (the
revised version of *Vakula*) but the triumphant
first performance itself on January 19th/31st,
1887. He had suffered 'indescribable mental
torture' all day and reached the theatre 'half
dead', but pulled himself together and conducted
successfully. This was a very different Tchaïkovsky from the man who had run away from the
Petersburg *première* of *Mazeppa* only three years
before. He followed up this conquest over his
nerves by another, conducting a whole concert of
his own works in Petersburg on March 5th/17th,

and began to think of venturing on a concert
tour abroad. 'My nerves are astonishingly
strengthened and things which were at one time
out of the question are now quite possible'. He
also felt renewed confidence in his creative power,
though he found that mere orchestration 'gives
me more trouble, the older I grow; I am more
severely self-critical, more careful, more fastidious
with regard to colours and nuances'. The score
of *The Sorceress* was actually not finished till May,
an exceptionally slow piece of work. As soon as
this was out of the way, Tchaïkovsky set off on
another Caucasian holiday, making the delightful
steamer trip down the Volga from Nizhny-
Novgorod, and spent June with Anatol and his
wife, and Modest, not in Tiflis but in the country
at Borzhom. He was delighted with the place and
worked only for an hour a day at the orchestration
of four pieces of Mozart's for the suite *Mozartiana*,
the realization of an idea that had been at the
back of his mind for two or three years. He
intended to spend the whole summer at Borzhom.

But in July he was suddenly called by telegram
from the borders of Asia to the other end
of Europe, to Aix-la-Chapelle, where N. D.
Kondratyev was dying. It was a useless sacrifice
on the altar of friendship, for Tchaïkovsky, sympathetic as he might be, was the most helpless
of practical friends. He was conscious of the
futility of his 'good deed', conscious that it was
done under moral compulsion, not spontaneously
from goodness of heart. He regretted Borzhom,

was bored at Aix—and all the time bitterly
reproached himself for his selfishness. Both at
Aix and at Maidanovo, on his return, he brooded
much over God, life, death and the ends of life.
He felt that in the end he had clarified his
religious outlook, but he was certainly unable to
express it very clearly. 'I should like to set down
my *religion* in detail', he wrote in his diary, 'if
only to make my faith clear to myself once and
for all, to define the boundary between it and
knowledge. But life keeps flying away'—a constant refrain of his—'and I don't know whether
I shall manage to express that *symbol* of the faith
which has recently developed in me. It has very
definite forms, but I don't make use of it when I
pray. I pray just as before, i.e. as I was taught'.

Tchaïkovsky was now called upon to sally out
into the external world again as a conductor, and
to a much greater extent than ever before. He
conducted the first four Petersburg performances
of *The Sorceress* (the *première* was on October 20th/
November 1st), then in Moscow a whole programme devoted to his works, including the new
Mozartiana (November 14th/26th). *Mozartiana*
delighted his Moscow audience, but *The Sorceress*
was a complete failure, a failure that 'wounded
him to the depth of his soul'. But these were only
preliminary skirmishes. On December 15th/27th
he set out on the main campaign, a campaign
which had as its object nothing less than the
conquest of Germany. In Berlin at the outset he
met Desirée Artôt, for the first time since 1869;

in Leipzig, where his concert-tour began, still more interesting characters—Brahms, Grieg and his wife, and Ethel Smyth—all at the house of his fellow-countryman Brodsky. Grieg charmed him. At first he and Brahms 'didn't really like each other'; each felt instinctively that the other disliked his music, so that their relations remained only outwardly cordial. But 'Brahms took great pains to be nice to me' and Tchaïkovsky soon found him 'very pleasant'. He appears to have been a little puzzled by 'Miss Smyth', however. This memorable meeting occurred on New Year's Day (N.S.), 1888. The next day, Tchaïkovsky had to face the Gewandhaus Orchestra for the first rehearsal and on January 4th he conducted his First Suite, which was received very well by the public though rather critically by the press.

Before going on to Hamburg, Tchaïkovsky rested for a few days at Lübeck, where he learned that the Tsar had granted him a life-pension of three thousand rubles a year. In Hamburg he conducted a whole concert of his own works, with a Haydn symphony; he was fêted by the Philharmonic Society; and he was rather amusingly lectured by the eighty-year-old chairman of its committee, Theodor Avé-Lallement, who told the composer frankly that he didn't like his music— particularly the noisy orchestration—and that it was a pity his obvious talent had been ruined by his education in such a backward country as Russia. 'He implored me, with tears in his eyes, to settle in Germany'. Tchaïkovsky took a

charming revenge on the old man by dedicating
his next Symphony (the Fifth) to him. After
Hamburg, Berlin. Then Prague. Passing through
Leipzig again on his way to the Bohemian capital,
Tchaïkovsky was honoured by a serenade, or
rather aubade, from a German military band
which, in spite of the anti-Russian feeling just
aroused by a speech of Bismarck's, played under
his hotel window early in the morning, awakening
him with 'God preserve the Tsar'. In Prague,
on the other hand, Tchaïkovsky's visit was made
the excuse for Pan-Slav demonstrations; the ten
days he spent there (February 12th to 22nd, N.S.)
were one prolonged ovation, not so much to
Tchaïkovsky's music, perhaps, as to a great Slav
artist. His two concerts were mere episodes in a
round of addresses, serenades and presentations.
When he was shown the Town Hall, the city
fathers, who were in session, rose as one man to
greet him. In Paris also, where he went from
Prague, conducting twice at the Châtelet, political
considerations did much to increase the warmth of
his reception. But in London, where he conducted his Serenade for strings and the Variations
from his Third Suite at a Royal Philharmonic
concert, his very considerable success must have
been entirely musical. Francesco Berger, the
Society's secretary, organized a dinner in his
honour. Otherwise his four-day visit was completely ignored from a social point of view.

After all these excitements, Tchaïkovsky returned to Russia in March and, after a visit to

Tiflis, settled in a new home at Frolovskoe,
between Klin and Moscow. The house was
smaller than that at Maidanovo, but more
secluded and amid infinitely more beautiful
surroundings. He felt no inclination to work and
again wondered if he had written himself out.
'Still, I'm hoping gradually to collect material
for a symphony'. In the meantime he, literally,
cultivated his garden. But he was 'dreadfully
anxious to prove both to others and to myself that
I've not yet *sung myself out*'. The new Symphony
(No. 5 in E minor) was begun in June 'with great
difficulty', though 'inspiration seemed to come'
later, and finished by the middle of August, being
immediately followed by the overture-fantasia,
Hamlet (dedicated to Grieg). Tchaïkovsky conducted the Symphony in Petersburg on November
5th/17th, 1888, and again a week later, with
Hamlet, at an R.M.S. concert. Then after a flying
visit to Prague, for the production of *Onegin* and a
performance of the Symphony, the Symphony was
given again in Moscow. But the composer was
profoundly dissatisfied with it. 'There is something repellent about it; a patchiness and in-
sincerity and "manufacturedness" which the
public instinctively recognizes. . . . Am I really
done for already?'

It seemed not, for immediately after his return
from Prague in December he took in hand a
ballet, *The Sleeping Beauty*, commissioned by
Vsevolozhsky, the Director of the Imperial
Theatres, who himself prepared a scenario from

Perrault. Tchaïkovsky worked at it with pleasure; the work went easily; and the whole three-act ballet was sketched out by January 18th/30th, 1889. Six days later the composer set out on a second tour of the West, making his first appearance in Cologne, where he was already attacked by violent homesickness. After that, he appeared in Frankfurt, Dresden, Berlin, Leipzig, Geneva and Hamburg. At Hamburg he again met Brahms, who stayed an extra day specially to hear the Fifth Symphony — and found it not unpleasant with the exception of the finale. Tchaïkovsky himself began to like the work a little better, but poor old Avé-Lallement was too ill to come and hear it. Tchaïkovsky spent the greater part of March in Paris, though without making any public appearance. There were to be concerts of Russian music there in June in connexion with the World Exhibition, but they were under the publisher Belaev's auspices, and Rimsky-Korsakov had been chosen as the conductor. Tchaïkovsky could hardly appear in rivalry and he was obliged to kill time before his London engagement on April 11th (N.S.), when he conducted his B flat minor Concerto (with Sapelnikov), and the First Suite. He left London for Marseilles early next morning, equally impressed by London's fog and London's orchestral players, and returned to Moscow by way of the Mediterranean, Batum and Tiflis.

Settling at Frolovskoe, Tchaïkovsky orchestrated *The Sleeping Beauty* during the summer and, curiously enough, although the actual composition had gone so quickly and smoothly, he again had trouble with the scoring. The new ballet, one of Tchaïkovsky's own favourite works, had its first public performance in Petersburg on January 3rd/15th, 1890, but the composer had already been deeply hurt by the Tsar's very restrained praise of his music after the gala rehearsal the evening before. A week or so later he left for Italy, which he had not seen for eight years.

In Florence he at once began to work at a new opera, *The Queen of Spades*, commissioned by Vsevolozhsky as what the magnates of the film-world call a 'starring vehicle' for the tenor N. N. Figner and his wife Medea, then at the height of their popularity. As it happened, Modest Tchaïkovsky had some three years before written a libretto, an outrageously sentimental and melodramatic caricature of Pushkin's ironical story, for another composer, N. S. Klenovsky. Klenovsky had refused to have anything to do with it, but the librettist's brother liked it and set it *con amore*. The mood of life-weariness in which he had come to Italy, indifferent to her sunshine and blue skies, quickly passed. He began to 'live in' the libretto so intensely that in writing the final scene he was 'suddenly overcome by such pity' for the unheroic hero that he burst into tears. The whole sketch was finished by March 3rd/15th. 'Speed in working is a most essential trait of my character! . . . I worked slowly at *The Sorceress* and the Fifth Symphony and yet they turned out badly; on the other hand, I finished the ballet in three weeks, and *Onegin* was written in an incredibly short time. The chief thing is—to write with enthusiasm. *The Queen of Spades* has certainly been written in that way'. 'Modi', he wrote to his brother, 'unless I'm terribly mistaken *The Queen of Spades* is a masterpiece'. Next to *Onegin*, it is certainly his most successful composition for the stage.

After a week or so in Rome, Tchaïkovsky returned in May to Frolovskoe to find to his consternation that '*the whole, literally the whole of the forest has been cut down!*' He had lost his favourite walks. But his garden brought him compensation; his flowers had 'never been so luxuriant'. 'I find more and more delight in the cultivation of flowers', he told Nadezhda von Meck, 'and console myself with the idea of devoting myself to it entirely when my creative powers begin to show signs of old age. In the meantime, I can't complain. I had no sooner finished the opera, than I at once took up a new work, the sketch of which is already completed'. This 'new work', the String Sextet (*Souvenir de Florence*), sketched in little more than a fortnight, clearly reflects the tranquil happiness of the spring and summer, a happiness soon to be shattered for ever.

CHAPTER VII

1890-93

IN September, 1890, during his now almost
annual expedition to Tiflis, Tchaïkovsky sketched
out a symphonic ballad, *The Voevoda*. (This had no
connexion with his early opera of the same name
but was based on Pushkin's translation of a poem
by Mickiewicz.) Before leaving Tiflis, however,
Tchaïkovsky received very unpleasant news from
Mme. von Meck. Only a couple of months
before, she had sent him a considerable sum in
addition to the annuity, but she now suddenly
informed him that she was on the verge of
bankruptcy and that consequently the annuity
itself, which then amounted to about a third of
his total income, would have to be discontinued.
'Don't forget; think of me sometimes', she added
at the end of her letter. Tchaïkovsky took this
sentimental little gesture with more seriousness

than it deserved. Reproaching her for suggesting that he might be ungrateful, he wrote: 'I am glad you can no longer share your means with me, so that I may show my warm, unbounded and inexpressible gratitude'. But despite these brave words, he was very worried at the prospect of having to 'start quite another life, one on a more restricted scale', as he told Jurgenson. 'I shall probably be obliged to look for some sort of well-paid post in Petersburg. It's very, very bitter—yes, bitter!' (As a matter of fact, his royalties from *The Queen of Spades* alone soon more than replaced the annuity.) The real tragedy came later when he found that Nadezhda's financial troubles were purely imaginary, the product of an imagination disordered by the nervous complaint of which she was slowly dying. But Tchaïkovsky now saw in the affair nothing but a pretext for stopping his annuity. 'My relations with her were such that her generous gifts never oppressed me', he told Jurgenson, 'but now in retrospect they weigh on me. My pride is wounded; my faith in her unfailing readiness to help me materially, and to make any sacrifice for my sake, is betrayed'. Worst of all, when he tried to resume the old correspondence as if nothing had happened, she completely ignored his letters. It would be no exaggeration to say that the ending of this strange, precious friendship completely embittered the two or three remaining years of his life. For the manner of the ending changed and vulgarized for him the whole of the past. He saw himself as the mere plaything of a wealthy, eccentric woman. 'I have never yet felt so lowered or my pride so deeply injured. . . . I would sooner have believed that the ground would give way under me than that Nadezhda Filaretovna would change her attitude to me. And yet the inconceivable has happened and all my conceptions of mankind, my faith in the best of it, have been overturned'.

Fate compensated him a little by minor kindnesses. Both the *répétition générale* of *The Queen of Spades* on December 6th/18th, at which the Tsar and his family were present, and the public performance the following day were definite triumphs. The Theatre Directorate at once commissioned a one-act opera and a ballet for the following season and, in addition to these, he undertook to write incidental music for a benefit performance of *Hamlet*. (It must be confessed that he did this rather perfunctorily, cutting down and rescoring his overture-fantasia, drawing on *Snow Maiden* for one entr'acte, part of the second movement of his Third Symphony for another; though the funeral march was a new composition.) During these visits to Petersburg Tchaïkovsky had become more and more friendly with the Belaev circle of composers, largely, of course, through Rimsky-Korsakov. 'He usually ended the night by sitting in a restaurant with Lyadov, Glazunov and others till about three in the morning', writes Korsakov. 'Tchaïkovsky could drink a tremendous lot of wine without losing command of his faculties; very few could keep up with him in this respect'.

For the subject of his one-act opera Tchaïkovsky chose a play by the Danish poet Herz, *King René's Daughter*, from which Modest prepared a libretto, *Iolanta*. But the subject of the ballet, E. T. A. Hoffmann's story *Nutcracker and the Mouse King*, was forced on him and he disliked it. Nevertheless he began the composition of *Nutcracker* before he started on his Western tour in March, 1891. This time he was going much farther afield than before. 'I have long dreamed of an American tour', he told Jurgenson. Now the dream was to come true.

The beginning was more like a nightmare. Even before he reached Berlin he was suffering from homesickness, 'the most agonizing thing in the world, for which the only remedy is—intoxication'. He was still homesick in Paris, where he conducted a whole programme of his works at a Colonne concert. And before sailing from Havre, he learned of the death of his dearly loved sister, Alexandra Davïdova, mother of that Vladimir ('Bob') who, next to his brothers Modest and Anatol, was probably the dearest of all living creatures to him and whom he made his sole heir.[1] His first impulse was to abandon the tour and return to Petersburg; but reflecting that that could do no good, he steeled himself and went on. He sailed on April 18th (N.S.)—and

[1] Vladimir, too, was a homosexual; he committed suicide in 1906.

the first day out one of the passengers committed
suicide. His nostalgia became so acute that on
the night of his arrival in New York he sat crying
in his hotel bedroom. But he was much struck
by the sincere kindness of the Americans and
soon convinced that 'I'm ten times more famous
in America than in Europe'. He was annoyed
that the critics thought it necessary to describe
his personal appearance and his behaviour at the
conductor's desk, but he got a remarkably good
press, even for his conducting. He visited Niagara
Falls and Washington, where he was a guest of
honour at the Russian Embassy, gave concerts
at Baltimore and Philadelphia — there were
four in New York—and sailed on May 20th
(N.S.), very weary, but very well satisfied with
his expedition.

Hastening across Germany, he reached home
early in June, returning to his old house at
Maidanovo, for Frolovskoe had lost its charm
since the woods had been cut down. At Maidanovo during the summer and autumn he
orchestrated his *Voevoda* and worked at *Iolanta*
and *Nutcracker*. While in Paris in March he had
made the acquaintance of Mustel's new instrument, the celesta, and fallen in love with its
'divinely beautiful tone'. He decided to use it
in both *The Voevoda* and *Nutcracker*. Asking
Jurgenson to have one sent from Paris secretly,
he wrote that he was 'afraid Rimsky-Korsakov
and Glazunov may get hold of it and use the
unusual effect before me. I expect this new

instrument will produce a colossal sensation'.
To that favourite nephew, Vladimir Davïdov,
on June 25th/July 7th, he announced that he had
finished the sketch of *Nutcracker*, adding: 'No,
the old chap is getting worn out. . . .' (This
was not, perhaps, mere playfulness; Tchaïkovsky
aged at this period almost beyond recognition by
those who had not seen him for some years; he
was 'old at fifty', says Anton Door.) 'The ballet
is infinitely poorer than *The Sleeping Beauty*—no
doubt about it. . . . When I'm really convinced
that I can set only *réchauffés* on my musical table, I
shall leave off composing'. His self-dissatisfaction
was so extreme that after the first performance
of *The Voevoda* in Moscow on November 6th/18th
he destroyed the score in a rage. (It was posthumously reconstructed from the orchestral parts as
Op. 78.)

The next month Tchaïkovsky set out on another
concert tour, beginning at Kiev. In Warsaw he
was overwhelmed with nostalgia again; the
production of *Eugene Onegin* at Hamburg, conducted by Gustav Mahler, cheered him; but
in Paris he was so depressed and homesick
that he abandoned the concerts he was to have
given in Holland and fled back to Russia.
The destroyed *Voevoda* was to have been played
at an R.M.S. concert in Petersburg on March
7th/19th, 1892, and Tchaïkovsky, feeling under
an obligation to give some new work of his own,
filled the gap by hastily orchestrating a few of the
best numbers from his new ballet and giving

them as a concert suite. Thus the *Nutcracker*
Suite was actually performed before the ballet.
It won an immediate success, every movement
but one being encored.

In May Tchaïkovsky made yet another move,
his last, to a house near the town of Klin itself.
(It was preserved as a Tchaïkovsky Museum, the
property of the Russian State, till it was destroyed
by the Nazi invaders.) In this new home he
began a sixth Symphony in E flat. But the composition was interrupted by a three weeks' cure at
Vichy and on his return to Russia his time was
taken up by a mass of proof-correcting. However, by the autumn the Symphony was nearly
finished. But it seemed to him 'an empty pattern
of sounds without genuine inspiration, written for
the sake of writing', and he destroyed it. Or
rather, he diverted it to another purpose, The
first movement was converted into a concert-piece
for piano and orchestra, the so-called Concerto
No. 3, Op. 75, while the *andante* and finale were
also recast for piano and orchestra but never
completed. In Taneev's orchestration, they were
posthumously published as Op. 79.

The winter was one of triumphs. *The Queen of
Spades* was given in Prague; the French Academy
elected the composer a Corresponding Member;
Cambridge offered him an honorary doctorate of
music; the Sextet, now revised, won an immediate
success and the composer was given the Petersburg
Chamber Music Society's medal. The only
reverse was on the occasion of the first perform-

ances of *Iolanta* and *Nutcracker* on December 6th/ 18th, for the success of the two new works was very moderate and Tchaïkovsky was proportionately downcast. 'When one has been living for a long time in expectation of some important event, as soon as the event is over one feels a certain apathy, a dislike of any kind of work, and the emptiness and futility of all our efforts become all too obvious'. It was in that mood of self-disillusionment that he abandoned the nearly finished E flat Symphony.

A week after the unlucky double *première* he went abroad, first to Montbeillard to see his old governess, Fanny Dürbach, whom he had only recently discovered to be still alive. At Basel on the way he had 'fits of crying', agonizing home-sickness which grew worse every time he left Russia for no matter how short a period. But the meeting with 'Mlle. Fanny' cheered him; he gave a 'brilliant concert' in Brussels; and on his return to Russia in January, 1893, he was fêted for more than a week at Odessa. (It was during this visit to Odessa that Kuznetsov painted the well-known portrait, of which Modest says: 'There is no more living picture of my brother in existence'.)

The 'worn out', 'done for' composer was already at work again directly after his return to Klin. 'During the journey, I got hold of the idea for a new symphony', he writes on February 11th/ 23rd to Vladimir Davïdov, to whom he dedicated the work. 'This time a programme-symphony, but with a programme which shall remain an enigma for everyone—let them puzzle their heads over it. The symphony will be called simply "Programme Symphony" (No. 6). This programme is subjective through and through, and during my journey, while composing it in my mind, I often wept bitterly. On my return I set to work at the sketches and worked with such fire and rapidity that the first movement was quite finished in less than four days, while the other movements are clearly defined in my thoughts. . . . The finale will be a very long-drawn adagio. . . . You can't think what a delight it is to feel that my time is not yet over'.

He could even relax in a couple of dozen songs and piano pieces (Opp. 72 and 73) written for Jurgenson, and a military march for the 98th Infantry Regiment, commanded by his cousin, Andrey Tchaïkovsky. In March he was fêted at Kharkov, and in May came the still greater English triumph, though a triumph shot through with terrible nostalgia 'not to be described in words (there is a passage in my new Symphony which, I feel, adequately expresses it)'. He arrived in London on May 29th (N.S.) and conducted his Fourth Symphony at a Royal Philharmonic Concert on June 1st ('a real triumph'). There was a concert at Cambridge on the 12th, and the next day he received the degree in company with Saint-Saëns, Boïto, Grieg and Max Bruch.

At home once more, he resumed work on the

Sixth Symphony. The orchestration again gave
him much trouble, but it was finished on August
12th/24th, and after a short visit to Anatol he
began the scoring of the new Piano Concerto, the
original first movement of the discarded symphony. He was very pleased with the new
Symphony, except the finale, which he thought
he might ultimately replace by another. On
October 10th/22nd he arrived in Petersburg in
excellent spirits to rehearse the new Symphony for
the first R.M.S. concert of the season, six days
later. The success was moderate, no more. The
morning after the concert Modest, with whom he
was staying, found him puzzling over the question
of a title. He had given up the idea of calling
the work a 'Programme Symphony'—'Why
"programme symphony", when I'm not going to
give the programme?'—and it had been played
the night before simply as a 'Symphony in B
minor', though it was generally rumoured that
it 'had a secret programme'.[1] Modest first
suggested that he should call it a 'Tragic Symphony', a title which his brother rejected. Then
he thought of *Pathétique*. The composer accepted
this at once, wrote it on the score and sent the
manuscript immediately to Jurgenson. But the
very next day he changed his mind and wrote

---

[1] Some years ago what appears to be a rough draft of the
'secret programme' was found among Tchaïkovsky's papers at
Klin: 'The ultimate essence of the plan of the symphony is
LIFE. First part—all impulsive passion, confidence, thirst for
activity. Must be short. (Finale DEATH—result of collapse.)
Second part love; third disappointments; fourth ends dying
away (also short)'. Obviously this was somewhat modified later.

asking that the Symphony should be published
simply as 'No. 6'.

On the evening of October 20th/November 1st,
Tchaïkovsky dined with his old friend, Vera
Davïdova, went to the theatre, and afterwards sat
drinking in a restaurant till two in the morning
with Modest, two of their nephews, Glazunov and
one or two others. Next morning he complained
of indigestion and insomnia, but went out for
half an hour. At lunch he ate nothing but
incautiously drank a glass of unboiled water,
scoffing at his brother's fear of cholera. Though
he felt worse later, he still declined to see a doctor.
But in the evening Modest sent for the brothers
Bertenson, two of the best physicians in Petersburg.
Tchaïkovsky was now very ill and said more than
once, 'I believe it's death. Good-bye, Modi!'
The Bertensons pronounced his illness to be
cholera and only once did there seem to be hope
of his recovery. After a day or two his mind
began to wander. 'He continually repeated the
name of Nadezhda Filaretovna von Meck indig-
nantly and reproachfully', says Modest. At three
in the morning of October 25th/November 6th,
after a momentary gleam of apparent conscious-
ness, Tchaïkovsky died in the presence of two of
his brothers, his favourite nephew and the doctors.

Twelve days later Napravnik conducted a
performance of the Sixth Symphony which naturally, under the circumstances, made a profound
impression and, no doubt, gave rise to the legend
of the 'prophetic' nature of the last movement

and of Tchaïkovsky's 'suicide'. Whether he did actually commit suicide as he had threatened, and once before attempted, 'so that it would seem like a natural death', we shall probably never know. The drinking of unboiled water does arouse one's suspicion, but we have no right to treat that suspicion as anything more definite.

It is not without interest that Nadezhda von Meck died less than three months after the man she had helped so generously and wounded so cruelly.

.   .   .   .

It is customary not to criticize Tchaïkovsky's music but to sniff at it, or to admire the tunes. One either likes it or one doesn't. Yet an extraordinarily large proportion of his music—probably nearly two-thirds of it—is absolutely unknown in this country, even to intelligent musicians, while anything worth calling criticism of Tchaïkovsky is practically non-existent, except in the U.S.S.R.

The true nature of Tchaïkovsky's musical gifts is most easily studied from his earlier works. From these we see that he had a genuine lyrical talent, spontaneous, but easily lapsing into the commonplace and often *forced* into it by the pressure he put upon himself to keep on producing. His orchestration was always colourful in a crude, garish way, and it became rather more refined later. As a symphonic architect he was, from first to last, as inferior to Borodin as he was superior to Rimsky-Korsakov; in other words, he was able to develop organic sections but not organic wholes. Taneev summed up the nature of Tchaïkovsky's music in general with deadly accuracy when he spoke of the Fourth Symphony as 'ballet music'.

All Tchaïkovsky's earlier works are as objective as those of most Russian composers; that is, they are either 'abstract' music, or frankly pictorial or programmatic. And it was some time before his growing subjectivity—the inevitable consequence of unrelieved introspection—really began to show itself in his music. It conditioned his choice of subjects, limiting him in opera, for instance, to dramas in which he could identify himself with a principal character and contemplate the whole action from that limited point of view (above all, in *Eugene Onegin*). It suggested a 'subjective' programme for the Fourth Symphony. But the programme remains external, like any literary programme; it does not affect the tissue of the musical thought. The 'Fate' of the Fourth Symphony is a mere lay-figure compared with the 'Fate' of the Fifth. But after *Onegin* and the Fourth Symphony—that is, after the fatal marriage with its consequent crisis—subjective emotion begins to force its way rather hysterically into the very stuff of the music. The essential material of Tchaïkovsky's musical mind remained the same, of course, but it was now brutally forced into a sort of expressiveness which it did not really possess. The quasi-ballet-tune no longer remained a pleasant, innocuous symbol of, say, 'desire'; the composer now really used it as the—

sadly imperfect—instrument of his self-expression;
and so we get things like the slow movement
of the Fifth Symphony and the second subject of
the *Pathétique*.   There is a curious contrast between
the Fourth Symphony, professedly subjective but
really very near absolute music, and the *Manfred*
Symphony of a few years later, professedly based
on an external programme but where (at any rate,
in the first movement) the composer has identified
himself with his hero and written music which,
successful or not, is intensely subjective.

It is probable that much of this music written
during the eighties served Tchaïkovsky as a
cathartic.   It is certainly this later, intensely
emotional music of his, with its effective colours
and pretty, obvious tunes, which has done almost
as much as the comparatively early B flat minor
Concerto to endear him to the musical man-in-
the-street—who seldom detects the essential false-
ness of the curious, self-deceiving, self-torturing
personality behind it.   But it would be no bad
thing if musicians in general would take the
trouble to discover the unknown Tchaïkovsky
and so get him in more correct focus.   I personally find the nationally flavoured early works—
The Oprichnik, *Vakula the Smith*, the *Snow Maiden*
music, the Second Symphony and the rest—far
more attractive than the later very familiar ones,
Natasha's never-heard arioso from the first act
of *The Oprichnik* decidedly superior to the well-
worn 'farewell' aria from *The Maid of Orleans*,
and *Fatum*—if inferior to *Romeo and Juliet* (another

early work and a generally acknowledged masterpiece)—not so inferior that it should never be
played, while *Romeo* is very frequently played.
Until conductors and singers and pianists nerve
themselves to break away from their hackneyed
favourites, the ordinary music-lover's impression
of Tchaïkovsky the composer will remain seriously
distorted. Unfortunately he himself has made
such exploration all the more difficult by his
terrifying industry, his insistence on talking
whether or not he had anything to say.

BIBLIOGRAPHY

THE basis of all biographies of Tchaïkovsky must always be his brother Modest's monumental three-volume *Zhizn Petra Ilyicha Chaykovskovo* (Moscow, 1900–2); the slightly abridged German version in two volumes is far better than the seriously curtailed and not always very accurate one-volume English version: *The Life and Letters of Peter Ilyich Tchaikovsky* (London, 1905). Another important Russian book is Kashkin's *Vospominaniya o P. I. Chaykovskom* (1896), reminiscences to which he published an important supplement in *Proshloe Russkoy Muziki*, vol. 1 (1920), a volume entirely devoted to Tchaïkovsky documents. Tchaïkovsky's *Diary* was published in 1923, his correspondence with Balakirev in 1912, with Taneev in 1916, with Mme. von Meck (in three volumes) in 1934, 1935 and 1936, with Jurgenson (vol. 1 only, so far) in 1938. His family letters were recently reported to be appearing. A bibliography of Tchaïkovsky literature published between 1917 and 1934 was printed in volume one of *Muzikalnoe Nasledstvo* (Moscow, 1935). Many valuable articles, both biographical and critical, have appeared in the monthly *Sovetskaya Muzika*.

The Tchaïkovsky literature in non-Russian languages is not very valuable. Perhaps the best German book is Richard Stein's *Tschaikowskij* (Stuttgart, 1927). In English there are only Edwin Evans's *Tchaikovsky* (revised edition, 1935) and Eric Blom's little 'Musical Pilgrim' on some of the orchestral works. *Beloved Friend* by Catherine Drinker Bowen and Barbara von Meck (London, 1937) contains interesting, if badly translated, skimmings from the first two volumes of the von Meck correspondence. Markham Lee's little volume on Tchaïkovsky's music in the 'Music of the Masters' series (London, 1906) is spoiled by factual errors.

TCHAÏKOVSKY'S COMPOSITIONS

ORCHESTRAL WORKS

OPUS NO.

76. Overture to Ostrovsky's *Storm* (1864).

None. *The Romans in the Coliseum* (1864–65) (score lost).

None. Overture in F for small orchestra (1865). (Re-scored for large orchestra in 1866.)

None. Overture in C minor (1865–66).

13. Symphony No. 1 in G minor (1866).

15. Festival Overture on the Danish National Anthem (1866).

77. Symphonic Poem, *Fatum* (*Destiny*) (1868).

None. Overture *Romeo and Juliet* (1869) (completely revised—new introduction, new close and much re-scoring—in 1870; cut, further revised and re-styled 'fantasy-overture' in 1880).

17. Symphony No. 2 in C minor (1872) (first movement entirely re-written, scherzo radically altered and finale cut, 1879–80).

None. Serenade for small orchestra (for Nicholas Rubinstein's name-day) (1872).

18. Symphonic Fantasia, *The Tempest* (1873).

29. Symphony No. 3 in D (1875).

31. Slavonic March (1876).

32. Symphonic Fantasia, *Francesca da Rimini* (1876).

36. Symphony No. 4 in F minor (1877).

43. Suite No. 1 in D minor (1878–79).

45. *Italian Capriccio* (1880).

None. Musical Picture, *Montenegrin Villagers receiving news of Russia's declaration of war on Turkey* (1880) (score lost).

49.   Overture, *The Year 1812* (1880).
None. Coronation March (1883).
53.   Suite No. 2 in C (1883).
55.   Suite No. 3 in G (1884).
58.   Symphony, *Manfred* (1885).
None. *Jurists' March* (1885).
64.   Symphony No. 5 in E minor (1888).
67a.   Fantasy-Overture, *Hamlet* (1888).
78.   Symphonic Ballad, *The Voevoda* (1891).
71a.   Suite, *Nutcracker* (1891–92).
74.   Symphony No. 6 in B minor (*Pathétique*) (1893).

WORKS FOR SOLO INSTRUMENT WITH ORCHESTRA

23.   Concerto No. 1, in B flat minor, for piano and orchestra (1874–75).
26.   *Sérénade mélancolique*, for violin and orchestra (1875).
33.   Variations on a Rococo Theme, for 'cello and orchestra (1876).
34.   Valse-Scherzo, for violin and orchestra (1877).
35.   Concerto in D, for violin and orchestra (1878).
44.   Concerto No. 2, in G, for piano and orchestra (1880).
56.   Concert-Fantasia for piano and orchestra (1884).
62.   *Pezzo capriccioso*, for 'cello and orchestra (1887).
75.   Concerto No. 3 in E flat (in one movement) for piano and orchestra (1892–93).
79.   Andante and Finale, for piano and orchestra (1892–93), orchestrated by Taneev. (Op. 75 and Op. 79 originated as movements of a Symphony in E flat.)

OPUS NO.
WORKS FOR STRING ORCHESTRA

48.   Serenade in C (1880).

None.   Elegy (for the jubilee of the actor I. V.
       Samarin) (1884) (afterwards included in
       the incidental music to *Hamlet*).

CHAMBER MUSIC

None.   Introduction and Allegro for String Quartet
       (with two 'cellos) (1863–64).

None.   Prelude for String Quartet (1863–64).

None.   String Quartet in B flat (only the first *Allegro*
       survives) (1865).

11.   String Quartet in D (1871).

22.   String Quartet in F (1873–74).

30.   String Quartet in E flat minor (1876).

42.   *Souvenir d'un lieu cher* (three pieces for violin
       and piano) (1878).

50.   Trio for piano, violin and 'cello (1882).

70.   String Sextet (*Souvenir de Florence*) (1890–92).

PIANO MUSIC

None.   Valse (*dédié a m'lle Anastasie*) (1854).

None.   Theme and Variations in A minor (1863–64).

80.   Sonata in C sharp minor (1865).

1.   *Scherzo à la Russe* and Impromptu (1867).

2.   *Souvenir de Hapsal* (Nos. 1 and 3, 1867; No. 2,
       1864–65).

None.   Potpourri on Motives from P. Tchaïkovsky's
       opera *Voevoda* (published pseudonymously
       as the work of 'H. Cramer') (1868).

4.   Valse-Caprice (1868).

5.   Romance (1868).

7.   Valse-Scherzo in A (1870).

8.   Capriccio in G flat (1870).

9.   Three Pieces (1870–71).

10.   Nocturne and Humoresque (1871).

19.   Six Pieces (1873).

21.   Six Pieces on a Single Theme (1873).

37*b*.   The Seasons (twelve pieces) (1876).

40.   Twelve Pieces (of moderate difficulty) (1876–78).

37.   Sonata in G (1878).

None. March, *The Volunteer Fleet* (published pseudonymously as the work of 'P. I. Sinopov') (1878).[1]

39.   Children's Album (twenty-four easy pieces) (1878).

51.   Six Pieces (1882).

None. Impromptu-Capriccio (1885).

59.   Dumka (1886).

None. Valse-Scherzo, No. 2 (1889).

None. Impromptu in A flat (1889).

None. Military March for the 98th Infantry Regiment (1893).

72.   Eighteen Pieces (1893).

None. *Momento lirico*, completed by Taneev.

OPERAS

3.   *The Voevoda* (1867).

None. *Undine* (1869) (only a few numbers have survived).

None. *The Oprichnik* (1870–72).

14.   *Vakula the Smith* (1874) (drastically revised as *Cherevichki* (*The Slippers*), also known outside Russia as *Les Caprices d'Oxane* (1885) (no opus number).

24.   *Eugene Onegin* (1877–78) (Ecossaise for sixth scene added in 1885).

---

[1] This is the work which Modest erroneously calls the *Skobelev March*, that being the title originally proposed by Jurgenson.

OPUS NO.

None. *The Maid of Orleans* (1878–79) (various altera-
      tions made in 1882).
None. *Mazeppa* (1881–83).
None. *The Sorceress* (1885–87).
68.   *The Queen of Spades* (1890).
69.   *Iolanta* (1891).

BALLETS

20.   *Swan Lake* (1875–76).
66.   *The Sleeping Princess* (1888–89).
71.   *Nutcracker* (1891–92).

INCIDENTAL MUSIC

12.   To Ostrovsky's *Snow Maiden* (1873).
67*b*. To *Hamlet* (1891).

OTHER STAGE MUSIC, FRAGMENTS OF OPERAS, ETC.

None. Fountain Scene from Pushkin's *Boris Godunov*
      (score lost) (1865?).
None. Vaudeville Couplets (1867) (MS. lost).
None. Recitatives and Choruses for Auber's *Domino
      Noir* (1868) (MS. lost).
None. Chorus of Flowers and Insects for projected
      opera *Mandragora* (1869–70).
None. Music to Ostrovsky's *Dmitry the Pretender*
      (Introduction to Act I and mazurka)
      (before 1870).
None. Recitatives for Mozart's *Marriage of Figaro*
      (1876).
None. Couplets 'Vous l'ordonnez' from Beaumar-
      chais' *Le Barbier de Séville* (1877?).
None. Duet from *Romeo and Juliet* (possibly a sketch
      for an opera on the subject and partly based
      on the fantasy-overture; completed by
      Taneev) (1881?).

OPUS NO.

None. Melodrama for small orchestra, for the *domovoy* scene in Ostrovsky's *Voevoda* (1886).

CANTATAS, CHURCH AND CHORAL MUSIC, ETC.

None. Chorus *a capella* on Ogarev's *Na son gryadushchiy* (1863–64).

None. Another version of the same, slightly altered and with orchestral accompaniment (1863–64).

None. Cantata (for four soloists, chorus and orchestra) on Schiller's *An die Freude* (1865).

None. *Nature and Love*, for two sopranos, contralto, chorus and piano (1870).

None. Cantata (for tenor solo, chorus and orchestra) for the Opening of the Polytechnic Exhibition in Moscow (1872).

None. Cantata (hymn) (for tenor solo, chorus and orchestra) for the jubilee of the singer O. A. Petrova (1876).

41. Liturgy of St. John Chrysostom (four-part mixed chorus) (1878).

52. Vesper Service (harmonization of 17 liturgical songs for mixed chorus) (1881).

None. *Moscow*, Coronation cantata for soli, chorus and orchestra (1883).

None. Three Cherubic Hymns (in F, D and C) (1884).

None. Hymn to St. Cyril and St. Methodius (based on an old Czech melody) (1885).

None. Six Church Songs, for four-part chorus (1885) (*Tebe poem, Dostoyno est, Otche nash, Blazheni yazhe izbral, Da ispravitsya* (trio with chorus), and *Nine sili nebesnïya*).

None. Chorus for the Fiftieth Anniversary of the Imperial School of Jurisprudence (1885).

None. *Nochevala tuchka zolotaya* (Lermontov) for mixed voices, *a capella* (1887).

None. Male Chorus, *a capella* (dedicated to the students of Moscow University (1887).

None. The Nightingale (*a capella* chorus) (1888).

OPUS NO.

None.   Greeting to A. G. Rubinstein (*a capella* chorus)
            (1889).
None.   Three *a capella* choruses (1891).

SONGS

None.   *Moy Geniy, moy angel, moy drug* (Fet) (1857–58?).
None.   *Mezza Notte* (Italian words) (pub. about 1860).
6.   Six Songs (1869).
None.   *Zabït tak skoro* (Apukhtin) (1870).
None.   Zemfira's Song (from Pushkin's *Aleko*) (1870?).
16.   Six Songs (1872).
None.   *Unosi, moe serdtse* (1873).
None.   *Glazki vesnï golubïe* (1873).
None.   *Khotel-bï v edinoe slovo* (1873).
None.   *Ne dolgo nam gulyat* (1873).
25.   Six Songs (1874).
27.   Six Songs (1875).
28.   Six Songs (1875).
38.   Six Songs (1877–78).
47.   Seven Songs (1880).
54.   Sixteen Children's Songs (1883) (No. 16
            written in 1881).
57.   Six Songs (1884).
60.   Twelve Songs (1886).
63.   Six Songs (1887).
65.   Six Songs (to French texts) (1888).
73.   Six Songs (1893).

VOCAL DUETS

46.   Six Duets (1880).

ARRANGEMENTS, ETC.

None.   Scherzo from Weber's Piano Sonata in A flat,
            Op. 39, orchestrated (1863–64).
None.   First movement of Beethoven's *Kreutzer* Sonata,
            orchestrated (1863–64).
None.   *Adagio* and *Allegro brillante* from Schumann's
            Études Symphoniques, orchestrated (1863–64).

TCHAÏKOVSKY 143

None. K. I. Kral's *Triumphal March*, orchestrated (1867).

None. Dargomïzhsky's *Kazachok*, arranged for piano solo (published 1867).

None. Dubuque's *Romance de Tarnowsky*, arranged for piano duet (1868).

None. Dubuque's polka, *Mariya-Dagmar*, orchestrated (1868?).

None. Potpourri on Meyerbeer's *Pardon de Ploërmel* for piano duet, by 'H. Cramer' (1868?).

None. Fifty Russian Folk-Songs, arranged for piano duet (1868–69).

None. Rubinstein's 'musical picture', *Ivan the Terrible*, arranged for piano duet (1869).

None. Rubinstein's 'musical picture', *Don Quixote*, arranged for piano duet (1869).

None. Stradella's aria, *O del mio dolce*, orchestrated (1870?).

None. Trio from Cimarosa's *Il matrimonio segreto*, orchestrated (1870?).

None. Dargomïzhsky's trio, *Nochevala tuchka zolotaya*, orchestrated (1870?).

None. Piano accompaniments for M. Mamontova's collection of *Children's Songs*, on Russian and Ukrainian melodies (1872 and 1877).

None. *Perpetuum mobile*, from Weber's Piano Sonata in C, Op. 24, arranged for left hand with fresh right-hand part (published 1873).

None. *Gott erhalte Franz den Kaiser*, orchestrated (1874).

None. Liszt's *König von Thule*, orchestrated (1874).

None. *Gaudeamus igitur*, arranged for male chorus and piano (published 1874–75).

None. *Slavsya* from Glinka's *Life for the Tsar*, simplified and linked with the former Russian national anthem (chorus and orchestra) (1883).

61. Suite No. 4, *Mozartiana* (three of Mozart's piano pieces and Liszt's transcription of the *Ave Verum Corpus*, slightly altered and orchestrated) (1887).

None. Fantasy Overture by H. A. Laroche, orchestrated (1888).
None. *Night.* Vocal quartet (S.A.T.B.) based on
the *Andantino* of Mozart's Fantasia in C
minor, K.475 (1893).
None. Sophie Menter's *Ungarische Zigeunerweisen*
(rhapsody for piano and orchestra),
orchestrated (1893?).
Piano transcriptions of some of his own
orchestral works, etc.

LITERARY WORKS

Translation of Gevaert's *Traité d'Instrumentation* (1865).
Translation of the text of the Page's cavatina from
Les Huguenots (1868).
Translation of texts of Anton Rubinstein's *Twelve
Persian Songs*, Op. 34 (1870).
Guide to the Practical Study of Harmony (1871).
Translation of libretto of *The Marriage of Figaro* (1876).
Translation of Italian texts of six songs by Glinka
(1877).
Text for a vocal quartet by Glinka (1877).
Autobiographical Description of a Journey Abroad in 1888.
*Short Manual of Harmony, adapted to the study of religious
music in Russia* (second edition, 1895).
Musical criticisms (collected as *Musical Feuilletons and
Notes*), parts of the libretti of his own *Voevoda,
Oprichnik, Eugene Onegin, Maid of Orleans* and
Mazeppa, verses for occasional cantatas, for some
of his own songs, etc.

DATE			